Think Like Lawyers, Speak Like Lawyers
Preparing for U.S. Law School

Preparing for U.S. Law School

Think Like Lawyers, Speak Like Lawyers

박희진 지음

한국문화사

Foreword

It is a pleasure to write a foreword for this exceptional work. Readers who have just opened this important volume need to know about it, and as a professor at a well-known department in which initial work for it was done, the Department of Second Language Studies at the University of Hawai'i at Mānoa, I am the right person to provide that information and background. In fact, this work was begun when the author was a graduate student at that Department, under my supervision. And who am I? — I am a specialist in various aspects of second or additional language teaching (pedagogy, instruction, and so on), active in the Asia-Pacific region since 1977, and a professor at that university since 1988. You are welcome to review my academic record through a glance at my webpage or checking Google Scholar.

Importantly for the present volume, I am someone whose professional concern extends, by way of democratic values and a philosophy of teaching drawing on an ethic of care, to marginalized groups and individuals, including those which Korean discourse (in English) refers to as "multicultural" people. And within the specialized subfield of applied linguistics known as "forensic linguistics", also as "language and the law", we can unfortunately see that such individuals are often short-changed, or all too often actually harmed, by the manner in which a dominant or mainstream legal system handles them, despite their additional language and cultural needs. This, despite the fact that lawyers and attorneys are professionals, which means they have both specialized knowledge and exceptional sets of values, for which society recognizes, trusts, and rewards them. Again most unfortunately, in many countries, that specialized knowledge is not extended to the additional language and culture knowledge that is in fact not just needed, but (from a democratic point of view) obligatory for individuals in a multicultural society. The question of course which follows is, do such individuals recognize the nature of the society they are part of, and their role and responsibility within it?

Let us go a little further. What sort of understanding of society, and what kind of teaching of, in this case English as an additional (that is, second) language would be appropriate to the above, in the case of Korea? Or in particular, in the case of Korean legal professionals who are seeking an advanced degree from an overseas university—which usually means one operating in English?

It is the opinion of the author of this book, who has both a degree in law and a graduate degree herself from an international university operating in English, that an appropriate framework is what has come to be called Critical Language Pedagogy. And I of course support this. The very specialized subfield of English for Academic Purposes known as English for Legal Purposes has delivered some instruction in this general area (in a very few locations) but generally has not taken the particularly democratic and supportive stance, towards marginalized or even multicultural individuals, that is implied by Critical Language Pedagogy. At the same time, I regret to say, the field of Critical Language Pedagogy has not often been able to convert its ideas into the material form so badly needed: the physical textbook. So the present volume constitutes a major step forward for both areas.

An indication of this necessary, important, and unusual version of English for Legal Purposes is the textbook's emphasis on developing critical thinking, and its use of ethically-charged themes and case examples, that include for example, 'cultural xenophobia'. As the author states, "The objective of this textbook is to help students think like lawyers and communicate like lawyers by examining possible problematic situations with a critical stance". Of course lawyers will confront problematic situations; as critically-thinking members of a democracy they must approach these matters alert to the possibility that the imbalances of power which unfortunately characterize our age and the countries involved here are what is bringing the problem into existence. They must have an inquiring, challenging, critically-aware state of mind if they are to perform their professional duties in accordance with their democratic values, as they should.

As the careful reader will soon see, this work is very practical. But also, it does not take anything for granted. We must (and the author does) start with figuring out what the actual needs of students are. It is that which drives the construction of the underlying syllabus.

Language specialists approaching this work should be interested to observe various key pedagogical features, including the use of "codes" – projective devices which allow the surfacing of students' views without the instructor or the materials dominating. They will also notice the author's careful work in setting up tasks and activities for active use of the language. This is a pedagogy of learning through use and action. No lectures should be going on here! Instead, the aim is for "critical dialogue" to be the means for raising students' shared awareness of issues, as they move through each unit towards a final extended role play or mock trial.

Specialists in English for Legal Purposes are indebted to the author for this path-breaking effort. As a language academic whose work could be grouped under headings such as 'critical' and 'transformative' I am grateful to the author for making concrete and forward- looking sense of ideas she and I studied together.

Graham V. Crookes, Ph.D.
Professor of the Department of Second Language Studies (SLS) at University of Hawai'i at Mānoa

Embarking on the journey to study law in the United States is a momentous step that opens doors to new opportunities, challenges, and perspectives. For Korean students preparing to immerse themselves in the American legal education system, the transition can be both exhilarating and daunting. This textbook stands as a crucial companion in this journey, designed to bridge the gap between Korean and American legal systems and to facilitate a smoother, more informed transition into U.S. law schools.

Navigating the intricacies of U.S. legal education requires not only a solid foundation in legal principles but also an understanding of the unique linguistic and cultural nuances that define the American legal context. This textbook offers a meticulously crafted approach to preparing for the U.S. legal environment, with a focus on equipping students with the knowledge and skills needed to thrive in this new academic setting.

Each chapter is tailored to address the specific needs of Korean students, covering essential topics such as legal terminology, case briefing, and the Socratic method of teaching. The book provides detailed explanations of common U.S. legal concepts, supplemented by practical, interactive exercises that mirror the challenges faced in American law schools. Through a combination of theoretical insights and practical applications, this textbook prepares students to engage confidently with the complexities of U.S. law.

The author is a seasoned language educator who has studied law in both Korea and the U.S. and understands intimately the challenges faced by international students. Her expertise is reflected in the book's comprehensive coverage and accessible presentation, ensuring that readers gain both a deep understanding of U.S. legal principles and the ability to apply them effectively.

In addition to academic preparation, this textbook also emphasizes cultural adaptation and practical strategies for succeeding in a U.S. law school environment. It addresses the nuances of legal writing, oral advocacy, and classroom participation, offering guidance on how to navigate these aspects successfully. The inclusion of landmark cases, real-world scenarios, and sample exercises helps students develop the practical skills necessary for excelling in their studies and future legal careers.

As you prepare to embark on this exciting chapter of your academic journey, this textbook will serve as a valuable resource, guiding you through the process of acclimating to a new legal system and academic culture. Hopefully this book will not only support your transition but also inspire confidence and ambition as you pursue your legal education in the United States.

Welcome to a transformative educational experience. May this textbook be a steadfast guide as you take the significant step toward achieving your academic and professional goals.

Warren E. Chung, Ed. D.
Former TESOL department chair of The Graduate School of Teaching Foreign Languages at Ewha Womans University

Table of Contents

Foreword 5

A. Plan 13

B. Outline 19

C. Textbook 23

» UNIT I

LESSON 1	GETTING STARTED	25
LESSON 2	HOW TO DEBATE	31
LESSON 3	WATCHING A VIDEO	41
LESSON 4	READING FISHER v. UT-AUSTIN (A)	49
LESSON 5	READING FISHER v. UT-AUSTIN (B)	55
LESSON 6	MOCK TRIAL CASE ANALYSIS	65
LESSON 7	MOCK TRIAL PREP	75
LESSON 8	TAKE IN ACTION	87

» UNIT II

LESSON 1	GETTING STARTED	95
LESSON 2	HOW TO DEBATE	101
LESSON 3	WATCHING A VIDEO	111
LESSON 4	READING KOREMATSU v. UNITED STATES (1944)	119
LESSON 5	READING KOREMATSU v. UNITED STATES (1984)	127
LESSON 6	MOCK TRIAL CASE ANALYSIS	135
LESSON 7	MOCK TRIAL PREP	147
LESSON 8	TAKE IN ACTION	155

D. Appendices   163

» APPENDIX A

SCRIPT UNIT I LESSON 3   165

SCRIPT UNIT II LESSON 3   166

» APPENDIX B

ANSWER KEYS UNIT I   167

ANSWER KEYS UNIT II   173

E. Teacher's Manual   177

References   238

A
Plan

1. Introduction

In a study exploring American influences on South Korean lawyers, Chisholm pointed out a trend in the Korean legal market where major law firms have sought to hire lawyers with English proficiency (Chisholm, 2013). Following Chisholm, the need for English for Specific Purposes (ESP) in law was explored in my study in 2022 through a series of interviews with Korean law professionals. In the study, participants revealed a persistent desire for learning English for legal purposes and professional training at law schools in the Unites States (Park, 2022). They commonly stated that there was lack of learning or training for efficient and desirable English communication skills as part of lawyering at every stage of their education (Park, 2022). Responding to the needs found in the study, which revealed implications for English for Academic Purpose (EAP) in law education, this textbook is designed to teach Korean EFL students using Critical Language Pedagogy (CLP), preparing them for special professional training for foreign lawyers and law students pursuing higher education (for instance, the LL.M.) in the United States.

The target learners are Korean young adults who are planning to pursue a law education in the U.S. and whose English proficiency is equivalent to upper intermediate independent users of English above B2 level according to Common European Framework of Reference (CEFR) for languages. The objectives of this textbook include developing debate skills in a program that incorporates CLP in a curriculum of 8 lessons per unit with a total of 2 units.

2. Method and Rationale

Constructivist theory sees "students as a member of a culture and as a creator of knowledge" (Richards & Rogers, 2015, p. 140). In accordance with this view, this textbook incorporates CLP in an English course using Theme Based Instruction (TBI) and Communicative Language Teaching (CLT).

For language learning, CLP is a way to prepare learners to be active citizens who apply critical inquiry to the status quo and seek out alternatives that promote freedom, equality, democracy and solidarity (Crookes, 2013). These values also happen to be the fundamental tenets underlying the constitutional laws of contemporary democratic countries. Therefore, teaching English with a focus on argumentation skills in the context of legal disputes corresponds to the pedagogical frameworks of TBI and CLT.

This textbook does not aim to teach subject matters in law, but it aims to provide students with a framework to learn and use language required in a specific professional field. This textbook aims to be used for a curriculum which serves students holistically by both satisfying institutional requirements and providing relevant content (Brown & Lee, 2015). Even though themes and topics are derived from real world events and actual court decisions, no actual knowledge of law is required. The objective of this textbook is to help students think like lawyers and communicate like lawyers by examining possible problematic situations with a critical stance, not to teach details about the U.S. legal system and its statutes. Students will explore language and basic knowledge related to U.S. Constitutional Law.

This textbook integrates a CLT approach with EAP through listening and reading-comprehension, taking notes for in-class oral discourses and discussions, and writing legal argumentative writings (Brown & Lee, 2015). This is to encourage the use of all four language skills, in particular, comprehensive listening, intensive reading, interpersonal interactive speaking, and genre writing, which are especially important for studying EAP (Brown, 2007; Harmer, 2011). Materials and activities aiming at the final stage activity In-class Mock Trial allow students to integrate all of the four language skills and explore the role of authentic language.

While emphasizing pragmatics, which is particularly important in curricula using challenging professional themes and topics in Law and English, this textbook focuses on fluency and accuracy through students' autonomous and strategic involvement in learning in *opinion-sharing* activities such as Food for Thought, *reasoning-gap* activities such as Mock Trial Case Analysis, and *role play* such as the In-class Mock Trial (Brown & Lee, 2015; Richard & Rodgers, 2015).

Among the nine components of CLP identified in Crookes (2013), this textbook incorporates seven elements in each unit: i) Units are developed based on the results of a critical needs analysis (Park, 2022) to determine what students should learn and what approaches should be taken. ii) Each unit starts with Food for Thought on carefully selected codes, "projective device[s] which allows learners to articulate their own, somewhat unpredictable interpretation of problematic situations relevant to their life" (Crookes, 2013, pp. 60-61). iii) Each unit presents critical content relevant to students such as issues like diversity and culture. iv) Each unit concludes with a mock trial which aims to fulfill the critical pedagogy criteria of action orientation. Although mock trials are based on fictional cases, it presents issues that are hopefully relevant to the target students' real-life interests. The mock trial aims to let students examine the complex aspects of real-life problems, an attitude inspired by CLP which considers the student as "a potentially active agent in society not merely as a worker performing tasks or a student studying the language" (Crookes, 2013, p. 55). v) Lessons engage students through dialogue with their classmates and teachers in Food for Thought sections for codes as well as mock trial preparations and exercises. vi) Discussion questions for Food for Thought and guiding questions for activating schema and brainstorming take critical stances in order to facilitate students' critical thinking. vii) All units are designed with language learning orientation through exposure to legal jargon, listening and reading skills for learning legal contents and topics, speaking skills during mock trials and in-class discussions for Food for Thought, and writing skills for constructing arguments and composing syllabi.

3. Expected Outcomes

As second-language-learning material, this textbook encourages students to think like mindful lawyers and communicate like lawyers when they use English. In other words, this textbook highlights how English is used in different contexts. Thus, this textbook draws students' attention to the differences in vocabulary choice, types of genre writing and speaking, and strategies in using all the four language skills (Crookes, 2013; Richard & Rodgers, 2015).

Firstly, students will improve all the four language skills in general by participating in discussion exercises. Secondly, by accomplishing interactive activities like Food for Thought and mock trials, students will develop communicative competence and debating skills and strategies. Thirdly, students will construct arguments using three modes of rhetorical appeals and distinguish ten logical fallacies in order to conduct genre writing as well as writing a syllabus of a court decision. Fourthly, students will improve comprehensive listening skills and intensive reading skills in order to build up basic knowledge in legal disputes. Lastly, students will be able to prepare themselves to be mindful lawyers in the future with English proficiency that can serve them through critical inquiry into the status quo and seeking out solutions. This can be a response to what Menis asserted while exploring the implication of critical legal pedagogy, referring to a Supreme Court Justice and a law firm solicitor in order to describe an ideal law student's aptitude: to be mindful of legal and social issues (Menis, 2016).

B

Outline

Unit	Theme & Contents	Skills	Vocabulary / Expression	Activity
I.	• Diversity (1) Are affirmative action policies for college admission constitutional? • Media Fisher v. University of Texas (Fisher II) Case Brief Summary Law Case Explained[1] • Precedent Fisher v. UT-Austin[2] • Mock Trial Can regional background be considered in college admission?	• Interactive Listening • Interpersonal Speaking • Comprehensive Listening • Intensive Reading • Guided Writing • Genre Writing	• Vocabulary constitutionality, rhetoric, logos, pathos, ethos, contention, rationale, circuit, amendment, holistic, feasibly, amorphous, dissent, enact, compelling, precedent, counsel, petitioner, respondent, rebuttal, counter argument, syllabus • Expressions May it please the court, your Honor, on behalf of ~, representing ~.	• Lesson 1 Analyzing Code about "Made in Korea" in restaurant signs • Lesson 2 The Art of Rhetoric by Aristotle & Three modes of persuasion • Lesson 3 ~ Lesson 5 Key legal terms & Useful words for listening/reading, Watch a video/Reading a passage, Comprehension Quiz, Food for Thought • Lesson 6 ~ Lesson 8 Mock Trial Case Analysis, Mock Trial Prep., Writing a script, In Class Mock Trial
II.	• Diversity (2) What are the roots of xenophobia? • Media Korematsu v. United States Case Brief Summary Law Case Explained[3] • Precedent Korematsu v. U.S.[4] • Mock Trial Can a state college exclude a certain foreign language from the second language tests for college admission?	• Interactive Listening • Interpersonal Speaking • Comprehensive Listening • Intensive Reading • Guided Writing • Genre Writing	• Vocabulary antagonism, nationalism, patriotism, tolerance, prejudice, xenophobia, segregation, integration, internment, convict, ancestry, vacate, indictment, uphold, withhold, comply, detention, evacuation, concur, contend, imperative, remedy, pro bono, suppress, discount, vigilant, accountability	• Lesson 1 Analyzing Code about Anti Hallyu campaign vs. No Japan campaign • Lesson 2 10 Logical Fallacies & Countering Logical Fallacies • Lesson 3 ~ Lesson 5 Key legal terms & Useful words for listening/reading, Watch a video/Reading a passage, Comprehension Quiz, Food for Thought

Unit	Theme & Contents	Skills	Vocabulary / Expression	Activity
			• Expressions Logical fallacies; Ad Hominem, Ad Populum, Ad Misericordiam, Faulty Analogy, Hasty Generalization, Post Hoc, Begging the Question, Red Herring, Slippery Slope, Straw Man • Countering Logical fallacies Your argument is faulty, because~. It is a faulty argument because~.	• Lesson 6 ~ Lesson 8 Mock Trial Case Analysis, Mock Trial Prep., Writing a script, In Class Mock Trial, Writing a syllabus

---

1 Quimbee. (2021, September 7.) *Fisher v. University of Texas (Fisher II) Case Brief Summary I Law Case Explained* [Video]. Youtube. https://www.youtube.com/watch?v=e6J1GNXzh-o&t=21s
2 Oyez Project. (1980). *Fisher v. University of Texas*. Oyez. https://www.oyez.org/cases/2015/14-981
3 Quimbee. (2023, October 13.) *Korematsu v. United States Case Brief Summary I Law Case Explained* [Video]. Youtube. https://www.youtube.com/watch?v=5O8Xsda2 AXk
4 Justia Law. (2003). *Korematsu v. United States, 323 U.S. 214 (1944)*. https://supreme.justia.com/cases/federal/us/323/214, Oyez Project. (1980). *Korematsu v. United States*. Oyez. https://www.oyez.org/cases/1940-1955/323us214, Immigration History. (2019, September 27). *Korematsu v. United States (1984)*. https://immigrationhistory.org/item/korematsu-v-united-states-1984/, The Administrative Office of the U.S. Courts. (n.d.). *Facts and case summary - korematsu v. U.S. United States Courts.* (n.d.). https://www.uscourts.gov/educational-resources/educational-activities/facts-and-case-summary-korematsu-v-us

C

Textbook

UNIT I

CONSTITUTIONALITY OF AFFIRMATIVE ACTION POLICIES USED IN COLLEGE ADMISSION PROCESSES

Objectives

- To develop critical thinking on issues related to diversity.
- To learn how to construct arguments.
- To learn and develop debate skills.
- To learn the conventions of a mock trial.

LESSON 1
GETTING STARTED

💬 Breaking the Ice

Take time to examine pictures below. Read the captions and think about your first impressions.

You may see signs like the one above at restaurants in Korea. They are notifications about the origins of the ingredients served at the restaurant. "국내산" means "Made in Korea." The signs above say that the owner and the employees at the restaurants are "Made in Korea."

The image on the left shows a variation on this practice. Next to the restaurant logo, it reads, "Since our restaurant is composed of pure native Korean people, they are more competent at Korean compared to other restaurants. Therefore, please use Korean when you order. The End!"

Food for Thought

» With your partners, share your feelings and opinions about these signs using the following discussion questions. Use the space below to take notes of your discussion and prepare a mini presentation for the class.

- **As a Korean**

  How do you feel about this sign? Is it simply a harmless joke? Why?

  What could be the original intent of the sign?

  How could this sign be changed to satisfy the designer's original intent?

- **As a foreigner**

  If you were a foreigner (or if you are a foreigner), how would you feel about this sign? What is your first impression?

Learning Concepts

The following words in the box can be used to describe the pictures below the box. Do you think these pictures can be described by a single word in the box? Or do you think the pictures relate to many words in the box at once?

- homogeneity vs. diversity
- majority vs. minority
- equality vs. equity
- race (racism)
- gender
- affiliation vs. disaffiliation

- Which word(s) do you think are relevant to the pictures below?

_____

_____

_____

Discussing the Concepts

» Compare your answers from the previous page with your partners. Are your answers all the same? Discuss why you chose to match those concepts to those pictures. Record your responses in the space below.

- homogeneity vs. diversity
- majority vs. minority
- equality vs. equity
- race (racism)
- gender
- affiliation vs. disaffiliation

	Matched concepts	Reasons

Review the Concepts

Fill in the blanks with the following words from the box.

- homogeneity vs. diversity
- majority vs. minority
- equality vs. equity
- race (racism)
- gender
- affiliation vs. disaffiliation

- It is not easy to compare ___(a)___ and ___(b)___. ___(b)___ means the quality of being fair while ___(a)___ means the state of being equal or having an equal number of something.

- ___(c)___ means the act or state of being associated or united.
- ___(d)___ means the act or state of cutting association.

- ___(e)___ means state or quality of being alike or same in kind or nature.

- ___(f)___ refers to any small group in society that is different from the rest because of their race, religion, or political beliefs, often leading to a lower social status. Meanwhile, ___(g)___ refers to the social group considered to have the most power in a particular place and sometimes the most members.

- In the past, in some countries, certain elements of an individual's identity such as ___(h)___ or ___(i)___ were considered to be socially and politically important because they could not be changed through one's own effort.

Our Real-life Issues

» Let's think about how you encounter the concepts we examined in this lesson on pp. 27-29. With your partners, discuss the questions below and prepare answers to the following questions to share with the class.

- When and where do you interact with people who are different from you in terms of race, gender, ethnic heritage, or other socioeconomic backgrounds?

- Have you had any experience where your race, gender, ethnic heritage or other socioeconomic backgrounds affected you either favorably or unfavorably?

- Do you think our own society is diverse? Why or why not?

- Do you think that our society needs to promote diversity? If so, what steps can we take to ensure diversity in our society? If not, then why not?

LESSON 2

HOW TO DEBATE

💬 Warm-up Discussion

With your partners, discuss the practice of debate using questions below. You may take notes for your discussion and answers.

- Which image above do you think best describes "debate"? Why do you think so?

- When do we engage in debates? Share an experience about when or where you participated in a debate, even as a spectator.

- What do you think the purpose of debating is?

- What are the differences between the four concepts below?
    - discussion
    - persuasion
    - argument
    - quarrel

- What skills might facilitate a good debate?

The Art of Rhetoric by Aristotle

- Previously, we considered the purpose of debate and the skills necessary for a good debate. Here, we examine ways to strengthen your debate skills.

- The famous Greek philosopher Aristotle (384 B.C.-322 B.C.) identified several types of argumentation which he called rhetorical appeals.

- Rhetorical appeals are "the qualities of an argument that make it truly persuasive."

- Logos
  - the appeal to reason

- Ethos
  - the appeal to one's reputation

- Pathos
  - the appeal to emotions

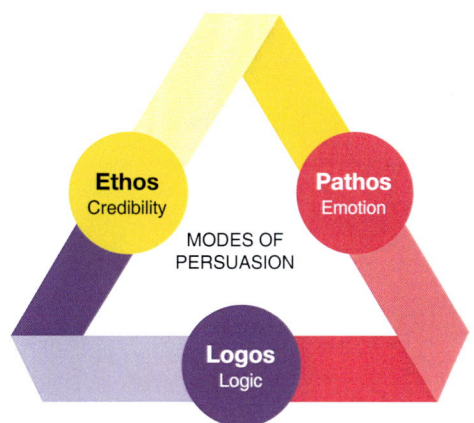

C. Textbook 33

Three Modes of Persuasion

» The following words in the box could be used to make different types of appeals. Fill in the table with the words from the box. Then, with your partners, compare your answers and discuss why your answers belong in the column you chose.

guilt, credibility, statistics, facts, love, fairness, experts' testimony, lust, self-esteem, law, trustworthiness, certificates, pity, belief in fairness, reliable sources, experiment, survey results, revenge, test score, analogy, anecdotes, scientific evidence

Logos	Ethos	Pathos
Appeal to logic or the reasoning ability of listeners or readers	The sense that a speaker or author gives as being competent, fair, or authoritative	Appeal to beliefs and feelings

Basic Argument Structure

The following table explains the elements of an argument.

Contention	Your main argument. Statements that must be supported with reasoning.
Rationale	Your rationale consists of reasons and evidence that support your contention. Logos, Pathos, and Ethos comprise reasons and evidence.
Impact	A brief conclusion by restating your main idea and ending with a powerful impression.

Analyzing a Sample Argument

After reading the sample argument below, i) draw a line matching a sentence to the elements of an argument on the right column and ii) find and underline supporting statements for each reason.

The death penalty should be abolished in Korea. First of all, it does not always effectively ensure justice. The death penalty is irreversible even if new evidence or judicial misconduct is discovered. Thus, innocent people may be sentenced to death. Secondly, the death penalty is inhumane since the right of life is the essential to one's dignity. Lastly, the global stance towards the death penalty is rapidly changing. By the end of 2021, two-thirds of nations in the world had abolished the death penalty. Abolishing the death penalty is one way Korea can demonstrate its dedication to global efforts to protect human rights.

- **Contention**
- **Reason(Logos)**
- **Reason(Pathos)**
- **Reason(Ethos)**
- **Impact**

Practice Using Rhetorical Appeals

» With your partners, discuss what could be a possible contention and rationale regarding the controversy on p. 25.

- State your position. See the given sample contentions below.
- You can use other ideas for each mode of persuasion in your rationale.
- Make sure that each point you make in your argument is supported by evidence or examples.

Example of conttention
The restaurant sign is acceptable.
The restaurant sign is not acceptable.

Example of rationale		
Logos **Rational appeal** Appeal to logic or reasoning ability of listeners or readers	**Pathos** **Emotional appeal** Appeal to beliefs and feelings	**Ethos** **Ethical appeal** The sense that the speaker or author gives as being competent, fair, or authoritative
Freedom of expression.	It is hilarious.	Most Koreans know it is not offensive.
Limit of Freedom.	Non-Koreans may feel sad.	According to human right experts, this can be seen as hate speech.

Construct your own Rhetorical Appeals

Using the space below, organize your thoughts and ideas based on your discussion on the previous page. Make sure that each rationale is supported by evidence or examples.

Contention

Rationale		
Logos **Rational appeal**	**Pathos** **Emotional appeal**	**Ethos** **Ethical appeal**
Appeal to logic or the reasoning ability of listeners or readers	Appeal to beliefs and feelings	The sense that the speaker or author gives as being competent, fair, or authoritative

Writing an Argument with Rhetorical Appeals

» Refer to the sample on p. 35 and your thoughts and ideas on the previous page. Then, construct your own written argument. Afterwards, you will share your writing with your partner and exchange peer feedback.

The restaurant sign

First of all,

Secondly,

Lastly,

In sum,

Peer Review

Exchange your written argument with classmates other than your partner and read several other arguments. Using the criteria below, read the arguments carefully to learn the various components that make up an argument.

Argument Identifier: #	
Criteria	**Yes / No**
Does the argument contain a contention?	
Is the contention sentence simple, straightforward, and easy to understand?	
Does the contention express a similar position to yours?	
Does the argument use all three types of appeals: logos, ethos, and pathos?	
Is the use of logos, ethos, and pathos clear and easy to understand?	
Are all three reasons of logos, ethos, and pathos supported by evidence and examples?	
Are the evidence and examples new ideas to you?	
Are the evidence and examples are relevant to each reason and meaningfully used?	
Does the argument contain impact?	
Is the impact strong and powerful?	
Are there any grammar mistakes or misuse of vocabulary in the argument?	
Additional comments and suggestions	

LESSON 3

WATCHING A VIDEO

💬 Before Watching the Video

Are you familiar with the term "affirmative action"?

» Check your knowledge of the words below. Choose and circle the best words or expressions that you think fit the meaning of "affirmative action". Then, fill in the empty box with how you think those words or phrases might help to define "affirmative action".

affirmative	action
"say, yes", supporting, positive, agreement, asserting, approving	movement, operation, policy, conduct, "do something", "a law suit"

C. Textbook 41

» With your partners, brainstorm at least two possible goals that an affirmative action policy might pursue in the space below. Refer to the given example.

To give opportunities to people from socially underprivileged groups.

Useful Words for Watching the Video

» Check to see if you know the words on the left. Then, with your partners, compare your understanding of the known words. Share your inferences for each other's unknown words. Use spaces in the table to take notes for your discussion.

	Known/Unknown	Meanings
affirm		
allege		
cert		
hold		
holistic		
index		
remand		

» Some words have different meanings in legal texts from ordinary usage. Check your previous knowledge of the following words on the left and match the words to the meanings on the right. Every definition in the right column will be used.

- **hold**

- **affirm**

a) to state something as true.

b) to have or adhere to a belief or opinion.

c) to confirm a judgement of a lower court.

d) to legally decide.

Using your best guess and what you learned from your discussion, match the words on the left to the meanings on the right. Check to see if your guesses actually correspond to the meaning on the right.

- **allege**   a) (as a verb) to send a case back to a lower court from which was appealed and (as a noun) the state of being sent back to a lower court.

- **cert**   b) something that directs attention to some fact or condition.

- **holistic**   c) to claim or assert something without proof.

- **index**   d) being certain.

- **remand**   e) dealing with or treating the whole of something or someone, not just a part.

Using what you learned, complete the following sentences below. Words may be altered for grammatical necessity.

> affirm, allege, cert, hold, holistic, index, remand

Tara was found guilty of driving under the influence at the District Court. She __(a)__ that she was innocent and brought her case to the Court of Appeals. The Court __(b)__ that the District Court's judgment was correct, but the sentence was excessive according to the new law for misdemeanors. So, it __(c)__ her case to the District Court. A month later, the District Court sentenced Tara with $3,000 fine instead of imprisonment and the Court of Appeals __(d)__ the decision.

C. Textbook   43

Key Legal Terms for Watching the Video

» The following concepts are useful when you watch the video on the next page. Read the passages below and discuss the questions below the reading passages with your partners.

• Strict Scrutiny

The Supreme Court analyzes Equal Protection cases according to different tiers of scrutiny. These levels of scrutiny are defined according to ways of i) understanding the government's goal for given policy and ii) the effectiveness of the policy in pursuing that goal.

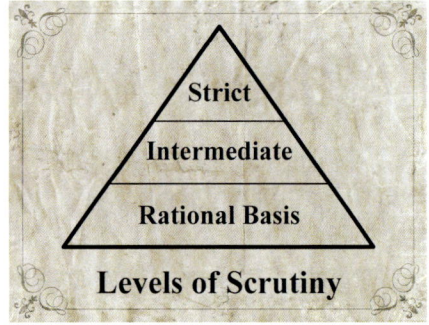

Q. What information in the passage do you think satisfies the idea of "strict"?

• The Fifth Circuit

In the legal context, circuit refers to a particular area containing different courts. The Court of Appeals for the Fifth Circuit is a federal court which reviews the cases sent from nine federal judicial districts including the District of Texas.

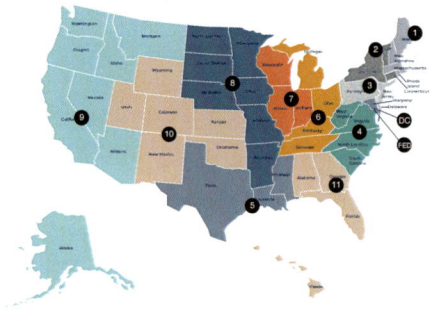

Q. Comparing your previous understanding about the meanings of "circuit", do you think the word "circuit" is an appropriate word to use for a group of courts and their judicial powers bounded by geography?

Watch the Video

You will watch a brief summary of a U.S. Supreme Court case. While you are watching the video, focus on the questions in the table below and take notes to answer the questions.

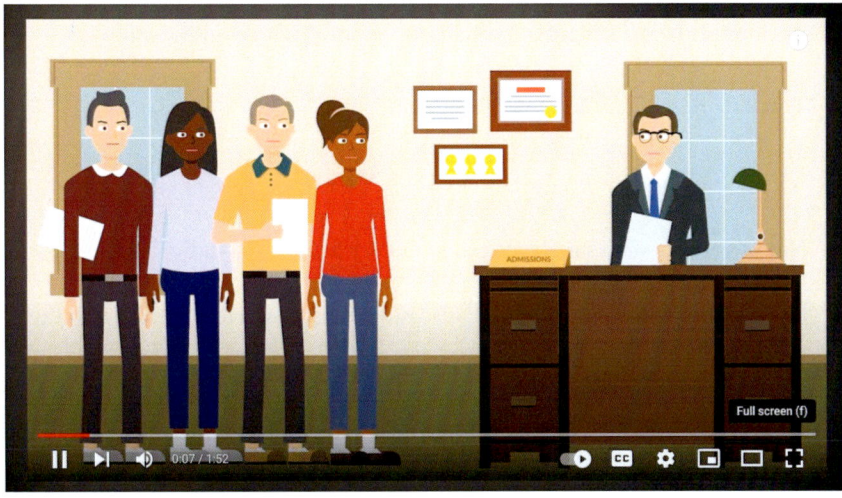

- Who is involved in the case?

- Whose interests are related?

- What is the main question in the case?

- Timeline

Listening Comprehension Quiz

» This time only the audio will be played. Listen carefully and complete the quiz below to review what you learned.

• True/False/Not Given

How do the following statements relate to the information in the audio?

True	The audio verifies the statement.
False	The audio contradicts the statement.
Not Given	The statement cannot be verified by the audio.

Q1. The university used two different standards to select qualified applicants.

Q2. Top 10 students of every high school in Texas enrolled in the University of Texas.

Q3. The Supreme Court decided that the university can consider race for admission decision but such a practice should survive strict scrutiny.

• Multiple Choice

Q4. According to the audio, which of the following statement(s) *CANNOT* be inferred?

a) Abigail Fisher graduated from a high school in Texas.

b) Abigail Fisher had argued her case against the university before the Supreme Court once before this case.

c) Abigail Fisher believed that she was discriminated against because of her race.

d) Abigail Fisher qualified for college admission based on factors other than her high school grades.

Food for Thought

Consider your own college application experiences. Discuss the following questions with your partners.

- What kind of qualifications do you think make a strong college applicant? Why?

- What are factors that you think are most important for colleges when deciding who should be admitted? Are there any other factors that should be considered in addition to academic accomplishment?

LESSON 4

READING FISHER V. UT-AUSTIN (A)

💬 Before Reading
How do we indicate parties in a case citation?

- The way of referring to the title of a court decision is different from the ordinary way of referring to competing parties. In the legal context, a "syllabus" also has a different meaning. The following example is the first page of a court decision that shows how we need to indicate parties in a case citation and the meaning of "syllabus" in the legal context.

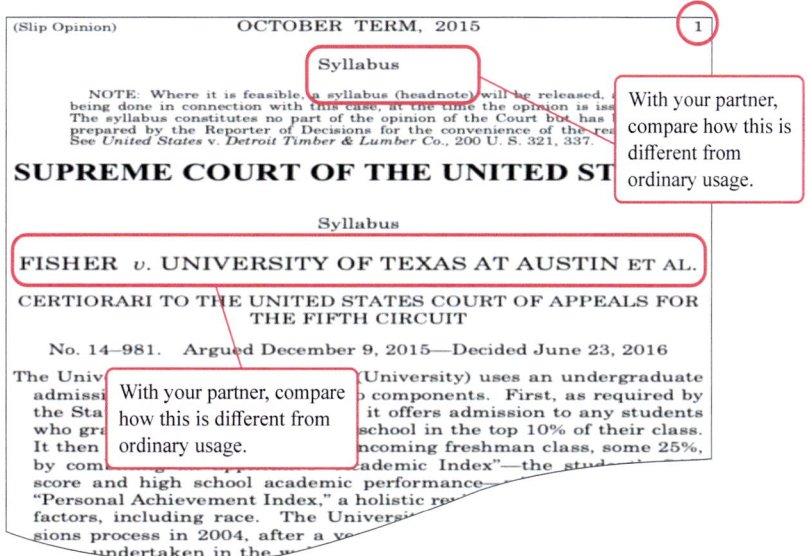

Useful Words for Reading

» Check if you know the words below. If you know the word, write the definition in the given box.

	Known/Unknown
amendment	
appellate	
tailored	

» Check your previous knowledge of the following words on the left and match them to the definitions on the right.

- **amendment**   a) relating to the appeals process, the process of changing an earlier court decision.

- **appellate**   b) made or changed to be suitable for a particular situation or purpose.

- **tailored**   c) an alteration of or addition to a motion, bill, constitution.

» Complete the following sentences with the words above. Words may be altered for grammatical necessity.

- The committee passed a new ___(a)___ of the bill to subsidize the living expenses of families who have adopted children. However, the President exercised the presidential right to veto the entire bill, alleging that the newly added provisions are not sufficiently ___(b)___ to the government's goal of promoting domestic adoption. Interest groups such as Children's Wellbeing took the issue to the court. When the district court ruled in favor of the interest group, the president appealed for a second examination at the ___(c)___ level.

Think Like Lawyers, Speak Like Lawyers

Key Legal Terms for Reading

The following concepts are useful for reading the passages in this lesson. Read passages below and with your partners and discuss what you think is the main idea or key information in the passage. You can circle or underline the phrases you think are important.

AMENDMENT XIV

All persons born or naturalized in the United States, and subject to the jurisdiction thereof, are citizens of the United States and of the state wherein they reside. No state shall make or enforce any law which shall abridge the privileges or immunities of citizens of the United States; nor shall any state deprive any person of life, liberty, or property, without due process of law; nor deny to any person within its jurisdiction the equal protection of the laws.

• Fourteenth Amendment

The U.S. Constitution includes twenty-seven Amendments. These are additions to the seven Articles in the Constitution. Many of these Amendments attempt to protect individual rights and liberties.

• Equal Protection Clause

Under the Fourteenth Amendment, the Equal Protection Clause asserts that states must treat an individual in the same manner as others in similar conditions, focusing specifically on fair and equal treatment.

Reading Passage

> Read the following passage carefully and prepare to answer the questions on the next page.

Abigail Fisher, a white female, applied for admission to the University of Texas but was denied. She did not qualify for Texas' Top Ten Percent Plan, which guarantees admission to the top ten percent of every in-state graduating high school class. For the remaining spots, the university considers many factors, including race. Fisher sued the University and argued that the use of race as a consideration in the admissions process violated the Equal Protection Clause of the Fourteenth Amendment. The district court held that the University's admissions process was constitutional, and the U.S. Court of Appeals for the Fifth Circuit affirmed this decision. The case went to the Supreme Court, which held that the appellate court had erred by not applying the strict scrutiny standard to the University's admission policies. The case was remanded, and the appellate court reaffirmed the lower court's decision, holding that the University of Texas' use of race as a consideration in the admissions process was sufficiently narrowly tailored to the legitimate interest of promoting educational diversity and therefore satisfied strict scrutiny.

The major question of this case was whether or not the University of Texas' use of race as a consideration in the admissions process violates the Equal Protection Clause of the Fourteenth Amendment. In a 4-3 decision, the U.S. Supreme Court held that the race-conscious admissions program in use at the time of the suit is legal under the Equal Protection Clause. Justice Elena Kagan did not participate in the discussion or decision of the case.

Source: Fisher v. University of Texas. (n.d.). *Oyez*. Retrieved March 24, 2024, from https://www.oyez.org/cases/2015/14-981

Reading Comprehension Quiz

Check your understanding by answering the questions below.

• True/False/Not Given

How do the following statements relate to the given passage?

True   The passage verifies the statement.

False   The passage contradicts the statement.

Not Given   The statement cannot be verified by the passage.

Q1. The Supreme Court agreed to the appellate court's standards as originally applied.

Q2. All the courts that tried the case shared the unanimous opinion about the constitutionality of the university's admission policy.

Q3. The goal of the admission policy of pursuing diversity contributed to the court decision.

Q4. Among the nine justices of the Supreme Court, only seven justices participated in the decision due to some of the other justices' shared interests with the parties of the case.

• Summarizing

Q5. Using words and expressions in the passage, complete the summary below.

- The issue of the case was whether or not Abigail Fisher was unfairly treated by a state university since it considered ____(a)____ of applicants. The Supreme Court ruled that such considerations were not violating the law of ____(b)____ .
However, when a court determines the constitutionality of this kind of case, a court needs to make the judgment according to ____(c)____ .

Food for Thought

» With your partners, discuss what kind of conflicts in terms of equal protection could be relevant in our day-to-day lives. Take notes and record your discussion and share your thoughts with the class later.

- Choose one issue below and think about anecdotes or cases you have encountered.

　• Gender

　• Race

　• National origin

　• Religion

- When did you encounter or were introduced to such a situation?

- Did your partners also have a similar experience?

- How did you feel about the situation? How did you react to the situation? Have you shared your feelings with others?

- If you had the authority, power, or capability to make any change to the situation, what might you have done?

LESSON 5

READING FISHER V. UT-AUSTIN (B)

💬 Before you read

With your partners, discuss the words below. You may start with guiding questions in the box. Take notes to share your thoughts with other classmates.

- Educational diversity
- State interest
- Life experience

- What do you think the words might imply? What could be included to explain the words?

    ex) *Life experience might include hobbies or criminal records.*

- How might those three ideas above be relevant to one's college admission?

    ex) *Life experience may stand for one's character that reveal whether or not one can study well at college.*

Useful Words for Reading

» Using your best guess and what you learned from discussion, match the words on the left to the meanings on the right. Check to see if your guesses actually correspond to the meanings on the right.

- **feasibly**

- **compelling**

- **amorphous**

- **dissent**

- **deferential**

- **demographic**

a) respectful; showing respect.

b) relating to the study and statistics of the population and social differences.

c) a strong difference of opinion on a particular subject.

d) possibly or plausibly.

e) having powerful or strong reasoning and being persuasive.

f) having no particular character, pattern, or clear structure; indeterminate.

» Some of the meanings of the words in legal texts can be inferred from their ordinary uses. Check your previous knowledge of the following words on the left and match the words to meanings on the right. Each vocabulary matches to two or three definitions in the right column.

- **precedent**

- **enact**

a) to put something in action.

b) any action or situation that serves as a guide or justification for future events.

c) to make law or to make an idea into a law.

d) to perform a story or play.

e) a decision about a particular legal case that makes it likely that other similar cases will be decided in the same way.

Vocabulary Review

Determine if the text is about legal contents or ordinary contents first. Then, complete the following sentences with correct words from below. Words may be altered for grammatical necessity. Words may also be used more than once.

- dissent
- deferential
- demographic
- compelling
- precedent
- enact
- feasibly
- amorphous

- Sophia had planned to collect a set of unbiased interviews. However, her method to properly select participants could not be __(a)__ carried out. Without considering __(b)__ diversity of interviewees, the interview results might mislead readers. The senior editor said that she needed to write an article with impartial evidence with little room for __(c)__ or arguing different points of view. Sophia thought his points were __(d)__ and she was __(e)__ when it came to his experienced advice.

- The show __(f)__ the life of Alexander Hamilton, a philosopher, a lawyer, and one of Founding Fathers of the U.S. It used dance and music, especially rap. It was a huge success on Broadway, but it failed to make a profit in Korea. Korean audiences might have found it hard to understand numbers performed in rap especially if it is about U.S. history and sung in English. This is unlike every other __(g)__ of Broadway musicals performed in Korea. Because of this, the unspoken rule that every Broadway show appeals to the Korean audience was proven false.

- In accordance with the implementation of a new law, the Supreme Court overturned a __(h)__ regulating the adoption of children from foreign countries. However, the minority opinion in the __(i)__ asserted that the newly __(j)__ law might violate UN conventions.

Reading Passage

> Read the following passage carefully and prepare to answer the questions on the next page.

The University of Texas' use of race as a consideration in the admission process did not violate the Equal Protection Clause of the Fourteenth Amendment. Justice Anthony M. Kennedy delivered the opinion for the 4-3 majority. The Court held that the University of Texas' use of race as a factor in the holistic review used to fill the spots remaining after the Top Ten Percent Plan was narrowly tailored to serve a compelling state interest. Previous precedent had established that educational diversity is a compelling interest as long as it is expressed as a concrete and precise goal that is neither a quota of minority students nor an amorphous idea of diversity. In this case, the Court determined that the University of Texas sufficiently expressed a series of concrete goals along with a reasoned explanation for its decision to pursue these goals along with a thoughtful consideration of why previous attempts to achieve the goals had not been successful. The University of Texas' Plan is also narrowly tailored to serve this compelling interest because there are no other available and workable alternatives for doing so.

Justice Clarence Thomas wrote a dissent in which he argued that the Equal Protection Clause of the Fourteenth Amendment categorically prohibits the use of race as a consideration in higher education admissions process. In a separate dissent, Justice Samuel A. Alito Jr. wrote that the majority decision was too deferential to the University of Texas' determination that its use of race in the admissions process was narrowly tailored to serve compelling interest and that the majority failed to properly apply strict scrutiny. Because the Fourteenth Amendment's Equal Protection Clause was enacted at least in part to prevent the government from treating individuals as merely components of racial class, race-based classifications, regardless of their purpose, must be subject to the strictest level of constitutional scrutiny. In this case, the University of Texas' use of race in its admissions policy cannot withstand strict scrutiny because the University's interest is not sufficiently and clearly defined and therefore judicial review to determine whether the policy is narrowly tailored is impossible. Even if it were, the goal of demographic diversity could only feasibly be achieved using impermissible quotas for racial balancing that are based on stereotypes.

Justice Alito also argued that the use of racial preferences is unnecessary to achieve the goal of diversity because the admissions process could use a race-neutral holistic review based on life experiences that would achieve the same effect. Chief John G. Roberts, Jr. and Justice Clarence Thomas joined in the dissent.

Source: Fisher v. University of Texas. (n.d.). *Oyez*. Retrieved March 24, 2024, from https://www.oyez.org/cases/2015/14-981

After you read

Determine where you can find the majority opinion and dissenting opinion in the passage on the previous page. Then, find information from the passage to answer questions in the following chart.

Majority Opinion	Dissenting Opinion
• Who joined the majority?	• Who joined in the dissenting opinions?
• Where do you find the contention?	• Where do you find the contention?

vs

Majority Opinion	Dissenting Opinion
• What are the reasons for contention?	• What are the reasons for contention?
vs	
• To whom is this opinion favorable?	• To whom is this opinion favorable?

» Refer to the sample in the box below. Identify contentions, rationales, and applications. Underline or highlight these phrases in the passage on pp. 58-59. In the margins, label these elements of argument. Determine what modes of persuasion are being used in the rationale.

Sample

The Court held that the University of Texas' use of race as a factor in the holistic review used to fill the spots remaining after the Top Ten Percent Plan was narrowly tailored to serve a compelling state interest...............
The University of Texas' Plan is also narrowly tailored to serve this compelling interest because there are no other available and workable alternatives for doing so.

• **Contention**

• **Rationale**
(   )

• **Application to the case**

» After reading the passage, has your understanding of the words below changed? Review your understanding of the words from your reading and fill in the table with your new understanding.

	Meanings
• Educational diversity	
• State interest	
• Life experience	

Reading Comprehension Quiz

» Check your understanding by answering the questions below.

• True/False/Not Given

How do the following statements relate to the given passage?

True	The passage verifies the statement.
False	The passage contradicts the statement.
Not Given	The statement cannot be verified by the passage.

Q1. The majority of justices determined that the university's effort was in accordance with a previous court decision about a similar case.

Q2. Both dissenting opinions agree that the majority opinion failed to apply strict scrutiny.

Q3. The Chief Justice was required to join the dissenting opinion.

Q4. Justice Alito believed that there are other methods to ensure a diverse student population without directly referring to race itself.

• Summarizing

Q5. Choose the best word options that could be placed in the blanks to complete the summary.

- The majority opinion determined that the university's consideration of race as part of its admission policy is not in violation of the constitutional law because it is narrowly designed to serve the state's ___(x)___. However, one of the justices voiced a(n) ___(y)___, arguing that using race itself as a factor in admissions goes against the intention of the Equal Protection Clause and another believed there might be other methods that could satisfy the goal of ___(z)___ without referring directly to race.

	X	Y	Z
a)	consideration	opinion	equality
b)	policy	decision	justice
c)	goal	concern	education
d)	interest	dissent	diversity

Food for Thought

Continue your discussion using the questions below and take notes on the key points.

- How do you think students' qualifications should be evaluated?

- Do you think such methods can effectively assess the qualifications of a prospective student?

- What do you think is the more important value to pursue in deciding college admissions: diversity or academic potential as measured by test scores or grades and why so?

LESSON 6

MOCK TRIAL CASE ANALYSIS

💬 Roles and Responsibilities

A mock trial activity allows you to practice your debate skills using rhetorical appeals in oral arguments at a court setting. Before we start, let's examine the roles of the participants in a mock trial in this unit.

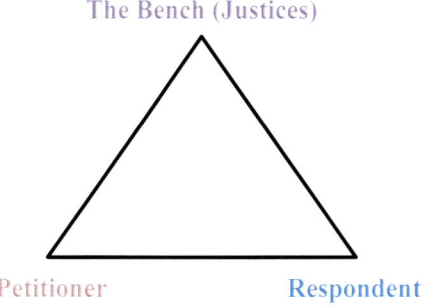

- The following table explains the parties for the mock trial activity in this unit.

Party	
• Petitioner	One who presents a petition to the court. A legal proceeding begins with a petition filed by a person who believes they have experienced injustice.
• Respondent	The party who is held responsible by the petitioner. The respondent defends themselves against claims made by the petitioner.
• The Bench (Justices)	The seat occupied by judges in the court who decide upon the case.

Mini Quiz!

What do you think the triangle implies about the parties' relationships? Share your thoughts. There is no right or wrong answer.

The Case

» The following passage provides the backgrounds and relevant details of the case that you will use at the mock trial activity. Read the passage and prepare yourself for the case analysis activities beginning on p. 69.

- Background of the case

Sara Noh is a recent college graduate who has prepared her law school application to a university in the country of Fairland. She has dreamed of becoming a lawyer in order to provide legal services to artists and entertainers in her hometown. In Fairland, those who want to be an attorney at law are required to graduate from one of the 12 national law schools and applicants can apply to a maximum of two schools during an academic year. There is one law school for each of the 12 different provinces. Sara applied to the Number One School of Law in a place called Province One, but her application was declined.

Sara was born and raised in Province One, which is a small town in Fairland. She attended schools up to high school in Province One, but she went to Supreme National University (SNU) in Supreme City, the capital of Fairland. SNU is the most prestigious school in Fairland with a 150-year-long history and has been ranked among the top 30 worldwide prestigious academic institutions by World College Ranking for the last 20 years. SNU requires a top 2% score on the Highschool Academy Competence Test. Sara majored in Magic at SNU and graduated Summa Cum Laude. In addition, Sara received 900 out of 1200 from the Legal Scholars Aptitude Test (LSAT).

Dani Winka immigrated to Fairland during his third year in college where he majored in law. His parents are political refugees from the People's Country of Cosmos (PCC). As soon as Dani and his parents settled down in Province One, Dani resumed his academic studies at a city college majoring in social science. Recently, Dani was admitted to the Number One School of Law through a special admissions plan that encourages local enrollment by giving 5% extra credit to applicants who graduated from a college in the same province. This admission plan was implemented in order to contribute to the government's goal of preventing population outflow from socioeconomically underprivileged local provinces. Population outflow from noncapital regions to the capital has been a serious social issue for the last 60 years in Fairland.

   Sara believed that the admission results is unjust.

Continues on the next page ☞

- Admission rubrics in the Number One School of Law admission brochure

Admission Rubric	Points(Total 100)
Undergrad GPA	25
LSAT	25
Study Plan Essay	25
Extracurriculars and Additional Factors	25

LSAT Score	Points
1200-1000	25
999-960	22
959-840	19
Below 840	16

- Timeline

2021 October	Sara Noh and Dani Winka applied to Number One School of Law.
2021 December	Sara's application was denied. Dani was admitted.
2022 March	Dani started attending the first semester of the law school. Sara filed a suit at a trial court in Province One. The Court held the court does not have jurisdiction for constitutional case.
2022 May	Sara decided to bring her case to the highest court of Fairland, the Supreme Court of Fairland which has exclusive jurisdiction over constitutional cases.

Case Analysis

After carefully reading the case brief from pp. 66-68, discuss the following questions.

- Whose interests are relevant here? What is the issue being debated?

- Who will argue against whom? Decide on who plays the part of the petitioner and respondent.

- What is the goal of the admission policy?

With your partners, discuss and compare the petitioner's strengths and weaknesses for admissions by using the information given in the facts and the admission rubrics.

Strength	Weakness

Case Analysis

» Read the Fisher case on p. 52 in Lesson 4 again and compare this case with the Fisher case to compare and contrast.

What is similar	What is different
Example *They are about school admissions.*	Example *Fisher case is about undergraduate admission and this case is about graduate school.*

Law for the Case

The following is the Law of Fairland. Make reference of the law in order to construct your argument in the mock trial.

- **The Constitution of Fairland** (Excerpt)

Article 10. All citizens shall be assured of human worth and dignity and have the right to pursue happiness. It shall be the duty of the State to confirm and guarantee these fundamental and inviolable human rights.

Article 11. All citizens shall be equal before the law, and there shall be no discrimination in political, economic, social, or cultural life on account of sex, religion, or social status.

Article 15. All citizens shall enjoy freedom of occupation.

Article 31. All citizens shall have an equal right to receive an education corresponding to their abilities.

Article 32. All schools and academic institutions shall enjoy freedom to work on educational programs to serve all citizens' freedom under this Constitution.

- **Act on the Law Schools Management and Administration** (Excerpt)

Article 22 Requirements for Admission: A person who has an undergraduate degree or who has equivalent academic qualifications under the Fairland Education Act may be admitted to law schools.

Article 23 Selection of Students: Law schools shall use the undergraduate grade point average, the test score measuring legal aptitude (hereinafter referred to as the "Legal Scholars Aptitude Test") and may use other materials that a law school may need to determine applicants' qualifications, such as community services and so on.

Organizing Your Thoughts for Ethos

» Referring to Law

Law will be the main source cited in your rationale. With your partner, examine p. 71 and discuss to determine what laws will be relevant to your argument.

Petitioner	Respondent
Example *The Constitution, Article 11* *: Petitioner shall not be treated differently because of their's education history since the Constitution prevents people from being discriminated against in terms of equal access to educational opportunities.*	Example *The Constitution, Article 11* *: The law prohibited discrimination on account of sex, religion, or social status. However, one's education history does not fit into any of those categories since it's not a social status.*

Organizing Your Thoughts for Logos

Referring to reasoning in Fisher v. UT-Austin

Even though the U.S. Supreme Court decision is not source of law applied in Fairland, it provides a reliable source of reasoning that could be used for comparison. Read the Fisher case on pp. 58-59 and your analysis on pp. 59-61 again and discuss how the reasonings in the Fisher case can help the petitioner and the respondent. Quote the reasonings that you choose and write down how they are relevant in helping either the petitioner or the respondent.

Petitioner	Respondent
Example	Example
A dissent of the Fisher case said "equal protection clause…"	*In majority opinion of the Fisher case "educational diversity…"*
or	*or*
A dissent of the Fisher case said that…	*Majority opinion in the Fisher case said that…*

Organizing Your Thoughts for Pathos

» With your partners, discuss how other factors can be used as pathos in your argument for either parties. You can use your creative ideas freely.

Petitioner	Respondent
Example *Petitioner is a hardworker.*	Example *Respondent put forth lots of effort.*

LESSON 7

MOCK TRIAL PREP

💬 Selection of Counsels & Justices

In groups of 3~4, you will take the roles of the petitioner's counsels, respondent's counsels, and the Justices on the bench.

1) Choose one person to be a team representative who will draw a role. (Roles will be changed in the next unit.)

2) As a team of the petitioner's counsel or respondent's counsel, construct your arguments together. Use the work for the case analysis in Lesson 6 on pp. 69-74.

3) Each team will be given 15 minutes in total. Each counsel on your team will present at least once. Allot time properly between counsels and prepare arguments accordingly.

4) If you are assigned to the justices on the Bench, decide who the Chief Justice will be. Prepare possible questions for each constructive argument and counter-argument.

» Case Info.: As discussed, complete the table below.

Official Reporter Citation	22-152
Caption of the Case	v.
Petitioner's Counsel	
Respondent's Counsel	
The Bench	Chief Justice Justices

Mini Quiz!

Why do you think lawyers here are referred to as counsels?

Hint. What word could refer to a person or people representing a single client?

Flow Chart of an Oral Argument

Remember the roles and responsibilities of parties on p. 65. Examine the flow chart and understand the tasks associated with each role.

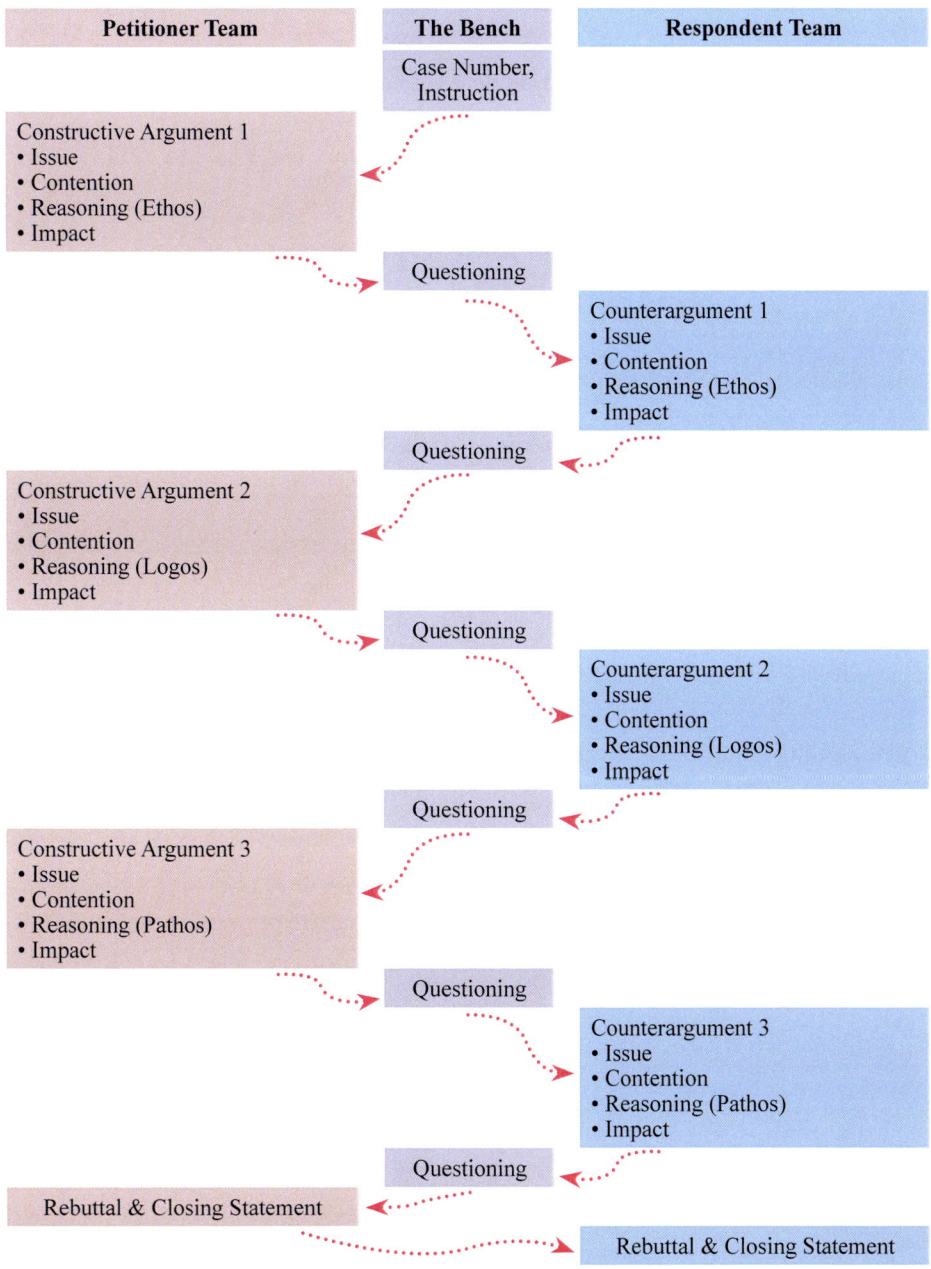

Elements of Oral Argument

On the previous page, you examined how oral arguments are developed during the mock trial activity. Let's examine what each task requires of you.

- Constructive Argument
  The purpose of the constructive argument is to clarify and support your position (in favor of petitioner).

- Counterargument
  The counterargument is a place for you to refute your counter party's position.

- Rebuttal
  Originally, a rebuttal means opposing the counterparty's argument using contrary proof. However, during the rebuttal, you can also

  1) recapitulate your overall arguments.
  2) make up arguments if you need since you spent assigned time answering the Bench's questions.
  3) add opposing opinions to the counter party that you couldn't include during your constructive/counterargument.

- Questioning
  During an oral argument, justices may ask the counsels questions about the particular aspects of the case and the counsel's legal argument

  1) to ask for clarification about facts and matters that are relevant to the law.
  2) to ask the counsels to restate arguments to persuade their colleagues at the bench.

Key Expressions in Oral Argument

An oral argument at court is not simply a speech presented to the justices at the bench. It is a dialogue between counsels and judges (justices) about the parties' legal disputes. Thus, certain styles and manners are expected in this formal setting.

Petitioner's Counsels	Respondent's Counsels	Justices at the Bench

"May it please the court" "your Honor" "on behalf of…" "representing…"	"May it please the court" "your Honor" "on behalf of…" "representing…"	"We will hear arguments for this case" "May I ask a question, counsel?" "The case is submitted."

- "May it please the court (and the members of the court)"
  - A formal introduction spoken by a counsel preceding an oral argument.
  - A ritual to show your respect to the court and the judge/justices.

- "your Honor"
  - The standard, formal way to address a judge in a court of law.
  - A judge, in any jurisdiction, is considered to be a person of honor. It is because the position of judge is supposed to be an honorable position treating parties and all people involved in the court system impartially according to law and one's conscience.

» What comes next is an adapted excerpt of an oral argument at a court. The dialogue refers to a fictionalized case. In teams, pick a role in the sample dialogue and take turns practicing the dialogue on the script.

Chief Justice

Today, we will hear arguments in Case 19-105 Niederman v. Drumptown, LTD .
I'll advise the lawyers that we grant fifteen minutes for each argument. If you don't spend the entire time during your argument, **we intend to grant** the parties the leftover minutes for the rebuttal at the end. **Ms. Petitioner's Counsel**, please go ahead.

Mr. Chief Justice, and may it please the Court: I am Sue J. Lee, appearing on behalf of petitioner Mr. Niederman.
The central issue here is whether or not Drumptown can evict Mr. Niederman because of his pet. *(Opening Statement, Addressing Issue)* First, Mr. Niederman should be able to keep his pet according to the law. *(Contention)* Article XX of the Constitution protects an individual's right to possess animals as a mean of private guard. Since his pet—the alligator—is being used to protect Mr. Neiderman, it deserves to be protected under Article XX. *(Constructive Argument 1: Ethos)*

Petitioner Counsel 1

Justice

May I ask, Ms. Lee, do you admit that Mr. Niederman is aware that the alligator is capable of causing greater harm than standard guard animals? *(Questioning)*

Petitioner Counsel 1

With respect, your Honor, Article XX does not make any distinction between types of animals and the amount of harm they may cause. Thus, there is no legal definition about guard animals. Coming back to what I was saying to conclude, Mr. Niederman is the one who has been wronged by Drumptown's unlawful eviction request. *(Impact)*

Chief Justice

Thank you, counsel. We will move on to next argument. **Ms. Respondent's counsel,** now you may start.

Respondent Counsel 1

Mr. Chief Justice, and members of the Court, and may it please the Court: my name is Kathy Young, representing respondent Drumptown, LTD. The petitioner misunderstands the central issue here. *(Opening Statement)* The central issue is whether or not Mr. Niederman and his pet—an alligator—violate the peaceful life of his neighbors. *(Addressing Issue)*
First of all, Mr. Niederman and his pet clearly violate the peaceful life of his neighbors. *(Contention)* Article II of the Constitution guarantees all citizens a peaceful life. Letting a vicious animal—an alligator—stroll around common areas such as a swimming pool is indisputably violating the other tenants' right to a peaceful life. *(Counterargument 1: Ethos, Impact)*

(ellipsis)

Continues on the next page ☞

Petitioner Counsel 3

May it please the court: I am Austin Kelly representing the petitioner. The eviction order by Drumptown betrays Mr. Niederman's trust in Drumptown's former behavior. *(Contention)* Three years ago, when Mr. Niederman moved into the condo, he inquired about Drumptown's pet policy. The property manager at that time replied that Drumptown did not have a pet policy. Placing strong faith and trust in that answer, Mr. Niederman has raised his pet peacefully for the last three years. Mr. Niederman is suffering from the shock of the sudden eviction order. *(Constructive Argument 3: Pathos, Impact)*

Excuse me, but Mr. Kelly, don't you think this pet is not any pet but an alligator? No matter how strongly you argue it is not harmful, to the general public's common sense, isn't it too obvious that Mr. Niederman's pet put other neighbors in fear and the amount of suffering of his neighbors' might be greater than his own?

Justice

Petitioner Counsel 3

In my experience, the population raising alligators has been growing in recent years, so even to general public's eyes, raising an alligator shouldn't raise irrational fears.

(ellipsis)

82　Think Like Lawyers, Speak Like Lawyers

Respondent Counsel 4

May it please the Court: I am Elliot Warren on behalf of the respondent. Today, I and my fellow counsels argued that Drumptown's request to evict does not violate Mr. Niederman's right. Instead, Mr. Niederman violates Drumptown tenants' right of peaceful life, putting them in enormous fear. Petitioner's counsels said that Mr. Niederman trusted that the property allowed him to house the pet. But, the pet—the alligator—has grown to enormous size. Recently, due to the huge size of the alligator, Mr. Niederman lets it out of his room and lets it stroll around common area in the building. The circumstances have changed. Mr. Niederman's way of raising the pet has gone beyond the general public's annoyance. In conclusion, it is clear that the respondent, Drumptown's, decision should be respected not only for the respondent's but also its tenants' favor.*(Rebuttal & Closing statement)*

Chief Justice

Thank you, counsel. The case is submitted to this court to discuss and make a decision

Preparing for an Oral Argument

» Oral argument preparation strategies
   1) Keep in mind the purpose of an oral argument is to persuade the justices in the bench to adopt your position.
   2) Know everything in the collection of your work to build up arguments with contentions, rationales, and supporting ideas. Clarify any questionable issues in the case and be familiar with relevant laws and similar legal cases.
   3) Prepare an outline of the oral argument that you will present.
   4) Be prepared for impromptu questions from the bench.
   5) Practice as much as possible and consider what makes an effective speech. Refer to the table below.

• Speech style check points

	☑
• Manner (proper use of respectful phrases)	
• Volume	
• Eye Contact	
• Gestures (body language)	
• Enthusiastic attitude	

Writing a Script for an Oral Argument

If you are on the petitioner or respondent teams…

- As a team, discuss and plan the ideas for contentions and reasonings.

- Then, divide into roles of counsel i) who will take parts of oral argument with reasoning ethos, logos, and pathos and ii) who will take the rebuttal.

- Make sure all the team members are prepared to argue against the opposing view.
    1) Each team member writes at least one script for their section of the oral argument and shares the outline of their section with all members.
    2) Fill out the table with your name as counsel and label it with your role and write a script.
    3) Use what you learned about case analyses in Lesson 6 and the argument structure in Lesson 2.
    4) For writing a script, refer to the sample argument on pp. 80-83 and make sure to use key expressions presented on p. 79.
    5) Refer to the speech style checklist on p. 84 and practice with your team members.

Counsel:	(Constructive/Counter) Argument

Preparing Critical Inquiries for Questioning

» If you are on the Justice Bench…

• Elect the chief justice. Then, discuss what kinds of ideas and thoughts will be critically questioned while each party's counsels are delivering their oral arguments. Use the space in the table and prepare a list of possible questions.

• What is a "critical inquiry"?
The term "critical" refers to a perspective that does not take for granted the existing state of affairs. Critical inquiry attempts to question whether or not liberty, equality, and justice is reflected in the counsels' oral argument. For example, "Is the party simply trying to reinforce existing hierarchies?"

1) Each team member should prepare at least two questions for the oral argument. Share the list of questions with the other members.

2) Use what you learned on case analyses in Lesson 6 to make critical questions. Try to find ideas beyond what you worked on while analyzing the mock trial case on pp. 69-74.

3) Refer to the sample oral argument on pp. 80-83 and make sure to use key expressions in the oral argument on p. 79.

4) During questioning, you can also request clarification about facts or a restatement of the argument.

Justice:	Possible Questions

LESSON 8

TAKE IN ACTION

💬 In-class Mock Trial

Courtroom seating layout

Arrange the classroom so that it reflects the U.S. Supreme Court courtroom seating layout.

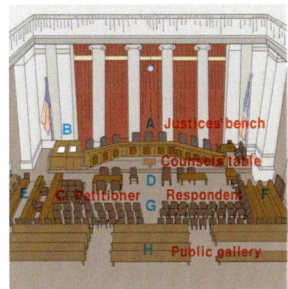 

Instructions
1) Take seats according to the Supreme Court courtroom layout.
2) When the Chief Justice calls the case citation and caption, the trial begins. The Chief Justice informs the court that each party has **12 minutes total for oral arguments** including responses to the Justices' questions. The Chief Justice informs the court that during the **3-minute rebuttal** at the end, each party can complete arguments that they haven't already finished.
3) At each turn for the oral argument, counsels stand up at the center of the counsel's table facing the justices at the Bench.
4) A camera and a screen will be placed behind the Bench to show the counsel's argument to other counsels at the counsels' table.

In-class Mock Trial

» Recorder: During the oral argument, take notes, recording the other party's arguments and the justices' questions.

Petitioner's Argument
Constructive Argument 1

- Contention
- Reasons
- Supporting evidence/example
- Impact

- Bench's questioning

Constructive Argument 2

- Contention
- Reasons
- Supporting evidence/example
- Impact

- Bench's questioning

Constructive Argument 3

- Contention
- Reasons
- Supporting evidence/example
- Impact

- Bench's questioning

Respondent's Argument
Counterargument 1
• Contention • Reasons • Supporting evidence/example • Impact
• Bench's questioning
Counterargument 2
• Contention • Reasons • Supporting evidence/example • Impact • Bench's questioning
Counterargument 3
• Contention • Reasons • Supporting evidence/example • Impact
• Bench's questioning

Peer Feedback

As counsels or as justices, you completed an oral argument. Now, take time to reflect on the process as a whole by working through this questionnaire.

Peer Feeback for Counsels

What did you think were the counsel for the petitioner's/respondent's strongest arguments?

Were there any surprising moments in the overall process of argument and rebuttal?

In terms of speech style, what were strengths of the petitioner's/respondent's counsel?

- Proper use of respectful phrases
- Volume
- Eye contact
- Gestures/body language
- Enthusiastic attitude

If relevant, please provide constructive feedback or suggestions for the petitioner's/respondent's counsel.

Peer Feeback for Justices

Did you feel that the members of the bench were able to maintain impartiality throughout the trial?

If not, why?

Were there any surprising moments regarding questioning from the bench?

In terms of speech style, what were the bench's strengths?

- Proper use of respectful phrases
- Volume
- Eye contact
- Gestures/body language
- Enthusiastic attitude

If relevant, please provide constructive feedback or suggestions for the members of the bench.

Personal Reflection

» In this unit, we examined diversity cases that might illuminate the conflicts in our own society. Write your detailed responses to the reflection questions below.

	Yes / No
Before this unit, did you feel that diversity issues related to your real life problems?	
If yes,	
If no, why not?	
How did completing this unit change your ideas about diversity?	
After completing the entire unit, has your position or attitude toward diversity issues in our own society changed?	
Based on what you learned in this unit, what would you like to change in our society?	

Writing a letter to the Ministry of Education

Assume that you already received the court decision in favor of your position. Imagine you are writing a letter to the Ministry of Education to suggest possible reform of college admission policies based on the Fairland Case.

Dear Secretary of Ministry of Education of Fairland

As counsel on behalf of   in the case,   v.

Before I represented   , I have believed that

After the court ruling, I learned that

I feel

Therefore, I hereby suggest

UNIT 2

CONSTITUTIONALITY OF INSTITUTIONALIZED XENOPHOBIA IN THE COLLEGE ADMISSION PROCESS

Objectives

- To develop critical thinking on issues related to nationalism and xenophobia.
- To learn logical fallacies and how to identify and counter them.
- To learn the conventions of writing court decisions.

LESSON 1

GETTING STARTED

💬 Breaking the Ice

Take a moment to examine pictures below. Read the captions and think about your first impressions.

Source: Korea Times Files. (2011).   Source: Kyodo News Images. (2019).

You may have seen scenes like those in the photos above in the media or might encounter these rallies when you visit either South Korea or Japan.

The photo on the left depicts a Japanese right-wing rally denouncing a Japanese television network that airs Korean TV dramas and shows. A sign in the photo says "Maggot TV*, Hallyu is brainwashing. Stop airing." (*a pun on "Fuji TV")

The photo on the right depicts a rally in Seoul, South Korea. Protesters condemned Japanese export controls as well as the historical issue of forced labor during the Pacific War. Protesters are holding signs saying that they will not consume Japanese products and they will not visit Japan.

Food for Thought

» With your partners, share your feelings and opinions about these scenes using the following discussion questions. Use the space below to take notes of your discussion and prepare a mini presentation for the class.

- Do you agree with the idea that watching foreign TV shows, using foreign products, or traveling to foreign countries poses a risk to our national identities? To what extent can foreign cultural products be considered brainwashing? You can share your own personal experiences.

- What factors might have led to these Korean and Japanese protests against each other's cultural products?

Learning Concepts

» The following words in the box can be used to describe the pictures below the box. Do you think these pictures can be described by a single word in the box? Or do you think the pictures relate to many words in the box at once?

- antagonism
- nationalism
- patriotism
- tolerance
- prejudice
- xenophobia
- segregation
- integration

• Which words do you think are relevant to the pictures below?

_____

_____

_____

Discussing the Concepts

» Compare your answers from the previous page with your partners. Are your answers all the same? Discuss why you chose to match those concepts to those pictures. Record your responses in the space below.

- antagonism
- nationalism
- patriotism
- tolerance
- prejudice
- xenophobia
- segregation
- integration

	Matched concepts	Reasons

Review the Concepts

» Fill in the blanks with the following words from the box.

- antagonism
- nationalism
- patriotism
- tolerance
- prejudice
- xenophobia
- segregation
- integration

- Regarding their dictionary meanings, ___(a)___ and ___(b)___ both mean devotion, love, and loyalty to one's own country. However, there is considerable difference between the two concepts. Depending on the context in which it is used, ___(a)___ is sometimes associated with ideas regarding the superiority of one's people and country based on hierarchical views regarding ethnic groups.

- ___(c)___ and ___(d)___ involve hostility or opposition. While ___(c)___ refers to an active opposition between unfriendly or conflicting groups, ___(d)___ refers to a fear of foreigners, people from different cultures, or ethnic groups. ___(d)___ could be caused by ___(e)___, which encompasses an unfavorable opinion or feeling not based in knowledge, thought, or reason.

- ___(f)___ refers to a fair, respectful, and permissive attitude or policy toward people whose opinions, beliefs, practices, racial, or ethnic origins differ from one's own or from those of the majority.

- ___(g)___ refers to the institutional separation of ethnic, racial, religious, or other minority groups from the dominant majority. ___(h)___ refers to an act or instance of blending with and becoming part of dominant culture.

Our Real-life Issues

» Let's think about how you encounter the concepts we examined in this lesson on pp. 97-99. With your partners, discuss the questions below and prepare answers to the following questions to share with the class.

- Can we identify any instances of xenophobia or nationalism in current affairs? Introduce the affair and share why you think it is xenophobic or nationalistic. If you cannot find any instances, you can start by discussing the following example.

  Ex) In a provincial city in South Korea, residents have protested against the construction of a mosque by organizing parties where Korean locals grill pork in front of the construction site.

- What might count as tolerance of the cultures, values, beliefs of people from other countries? Have you experienced tolerance or have you practiced it? How?

LESSON 2

HOW TO DEBATE

💬 Warm-up Discussion

In Unit I, we learned how to construct a persuasive argument with rhetorical appeals. However, do rhetorical appeals always guarantee a strong argument? With your partners, examine the picture below and answer the questions in the box below the picture.

- What rhetorical appeal does the man in the picture rely on?

- Do you agree with him? If not, why don't you agree with him?

Ten Logical Fallacies

» Logical fallacies are common errors in reasoning that are based on faulty logic. Logical fallacies will make your argument weak or even useless. Here, we examine ten types of common logical fallacies.

- **Ad Hominem Fallacy: a personal attack**
    - This is an attack on the character of a person rather than his or her opinions or argument.

Example

"You said we need to raise minimum wage, but it does not make sense since you don't have even a high school diploma."

- **Ad Populum: bandwagon justification**
    - An argument based on the assumption that the opinion of the majority is always valid: "everyone believes it, so you should believe it too."

Example

"The poll said that most of the voters in my neighborhood will vote for the candidate. Thus, I am going to vote for him too."

- **Ad Misericordiam: an appeal to emotions**
    - A fallacy in which someone tries to gain support for one's argument by exploiting the other party's feeling of pity or guilt.

Example

"I know the grade was given based on test scores, but please give me a better grade. I broke up with my girlfriend recently, I lost my bike, and I was diagnosed with Covid. I hope you take this into consideration and give me at least a C."

- **Faulty Analogy: false comparison**
  - This occurs when one assumes or asserts that two things are the same or equal while, maybe alike in some ways, they are not sufficiently similar to be considered equivalent.

Example

"Guns and cars are same in that both can cause deadly harm to human beings. If we need to control the purchase and possession of guns, it means that we need to restrict the purchase of cars."

- **Hasty Generalization: insufficient sample size**
  - This refers to jumping to a conclusion based on insufficient evidence or a sample size that is too small.

Example

"I know a tennis player who earns billions of dollars a year in prize money. I think you can make a fortune by playing tennis."

- **Post Hoc: false cause**
  - This is an assumption that the first event must have caused the second event.

Example

"The football team gets better grades than the baseball team; therefore, playing football helps you become smarter more than playing baseball."

- **Begging the Question: circular argument**
  - This fallacy is restating the argument, not proving it.

Example

"She is a good communicator because she has outstanding speaking skills."

- **Slippery Slope: one thing leads to another**
    - In this fallacy, a person makes a claim that one event will lead to another event until we come to some absurd conclusion.

Example

"Animal experiments diminish our respect for life. If we don't respect life, we are likely to be immoral and to careless about violence and killing. This will turn society into a battlefield. It will be the end of civilization. In order to prevent this situation, we should stop animal experiments right now."

- **Straw Man: misrepresentation**
    - This fallacy occurs when an argument is distorted or exaggerated and then attacked as if the exaggeration was the original claim

Example

"Proponents of sex education want to give kids freedom to have sex with no consequences."

- **Red Herring: diversion**
    - This refers to something that misleads or distracts from a relevant or important question.

Example

"The level of mercury in seafood may be unsafe, but how can we guarantee the fishing industry's profits?"

Identifying Logical Fallacies

» With your partner, discuss why each statement is a logical fallacy and write down the name of logical fallacy in the column next to the statement.

		Logical Fallacy
(a)	'Maggie and Beth have started attending fencing lessons. Fencing must be a popular sport in the country.'	
(b)	'The government should raise the minimum wage. People who don't agree with raising the minimum wage are selfish bourgeoisie who hate the working classes.'	
(c)	'You said we need to provide tax cuts to families raising newborn babies, but isn't this just because you are going to have a baby next month?'	
(d)	'British people who are taller and physically stronger than we are eat curry and chicken. If we want to raise our kids to be taller and stronger, we need to feed them more curry and chicken.'	
(e)	'Mineral water and Sprite Zero are beverages with no color and no sugar. They must have the same health benefits. I'd like to have Sprite Zero instead of mineral water.'	
(f)	'Considering his political attitude, if this candidate is elected, he will declare war against an enemy country and all of our sons and daughters will be recruited to kill and to be killed.'	
(g)	'Many of my friends at school travel to European countries to take a second language course and to spend summer vacation. So, I need to attend a French course in Paris this summer.'	
(h)	A: We need to raise the price of our products. B: If we do so, customers may leave. A: So, will you accept your salary cut?	

Countering Logical Fallacies

» Unlike casual day-to-day conversation, when you debate, pointing out the other party's logical fallacy is not only acceptable but effective in making your point. So, how do we point out logical fallacies in a debate?

- **Step 1:** Identify the error in reasoning.
- **Step 2:** Explain why it's not logical.
- **Step 3:** Provide a strong opposing contention and rationale. (Optional)

- Sample

  Speaker A   We need to spend more on stocking beverages like Sprite Zero. *(Contention)*
  Mineral water and Sprite Zero are beverages with no color and no sugar. Therefore, they must have the same health benefits. *(Rationale: Logos)*
  I'd like to have Sprite Zero instead of mineral water. *(Impact)*

  Speaker B   Your argument is faulty since it relies on a false comparison. *(Pointing out the error)*
  They may be similar in terms of color and sugar content, but they have little in common in terms of nutrition. *(Pointing out why Speaker A's reasoning is not logical, Rationale: Logos)*
  Mineral water and Sprite Zero should not be considered as similar to each other. *(Providing an opposing contention)*
  No expert agrees with the idea that we can substitute mineral water with Sprite Zero. *(Providing a strong rationale: Ethos)*

» With your partners, practice countering logical fallacies. Choose two statements from below and write a dialogue for each statement following the sample on p. 106. Take turns acting out the dialogue with your partners.

- "You said we need to raise minimum wage, but it does not make sense since you don't have even a high school diploma."

- "The poll said that most of the voters in my neighborhood will vote for the candidate. Thus, I am going to vote for him too."

- "I know the grade was given based on test scores, but please give me a better grade. I broke up with my girlfriend recently, I lost my bike, and I was diagnosed with Covid. I hope you take this into consideration and give me at least a C."

- "Guns and cars are same in that both can cause deadly harm to human beings. If we need to control the purchase and possession of guns, it means that we need to restrict the purchase of cars."

- "I know a tennis player who earns billions of dollars a year in prize money. I think you can make a fortune by playing tennis."

- "The football team gets better grades than the baseball team; therefore, playing football helps you become smarter more than playing baseball."

- "She is a good communicator because she has outstanding speaking skills."

- "Animal experiments diminish our respect for life. If we don't respect life, we are likely to be immoral and to careless about violence and killing. This will turn society into a battlefield. It will be the end of civilization. In order to prevent this situation, we should stop animal experiments right now."

- "Proponents of sex education want to give kids freedom to have sex with no consequences."
- "The level of mercury in seafood may be unsafe, but how can we guarantee the fishing industry's profits?"

	Dialogue #1
Speaker A	
Speaker B	

	Dialogue #2
Speaker B	
Speaker A	

Wrap Up Discussion

» What have we learned about logical fallacies? Consider the aspects of each logical fallacy. With your partners, discuss how we can avoid falling into logical fallacies in your arguments. Share your ideas with the class.

Ex) In order to avoid making faulty analogies, make comparisons that are highly similar or comparable in ways that are relevant to the point of your argument.

LESSON 3

WATCHING A VIDEO

💬 Before Watching the Video

You might be familiar with the Japanese surprise attack on Pearl Harbor on December 7, 1941. This initiated the U.S. entry into World War II (WWII). After examining the information below, let's explore how this person's life could have been affected by the events that he experienced.

- **Name**
  Fred Toyosaburo Korematsu.

- **Date of birth**
  January 30, 1919.

- **Place of birth**
  Oakland, California, U.S.

- **Occupation**
  Shipyard welder at the docks in Oakland.

- **Criminal history**
  Convicted guilty for violating military order in 1942.

- **Honors**
  Presidential Medal of Freedom in 1998.

Useful Words for Watching the Video

» Check to see if you know the words on the left. Then, with your partners, compare your understanding of the known words and share your inferences about each other's unknown words. Use the space in the table below to take notes for your discussion.

	Known/Unknown	Meanings
internment		
ancestry		
convict		
vacate		
uphold		
withhold		
indictment		

» Some words have different meanings in legal contexts and ordinary usage. Check your previous knowledge of the following words against the various definitions on the right. Guess the meaning of the words in the legal context. Discuss how a word's meanings in ordinary usage influence its legal meaning.

- **dismiss**
  - a) to remove someone from one's position or job.
  - b) to formally ask or order someone to leave.
  - c) to decide that something or someone is not important or not worth considering.
  - d) to formally stop a trial in a court of law, often because there is not enough proof.

- **motion**
  - a) a movement; the process of moving or changing.
  - b) a bodily movement or change of posture.
  - c) a proposal formally made to a deliberative power.
  - d) an application made to a court or judge for an order, ruling, or the like.

» Using your best guess and what you learned from the discussion, match the words on the left to the meanings on the right. Check to see if your guesses actually correspond to the meanings on the right.

- **internment**
- **ancestry**
- **convict**
- **vacate**
- **uphold**
- **withhold**
- **indictment**

a) to confirm or support something which has been questioned.

b) to deprive of validity.

c) to keep something that is due to or desired by another to oneself rather than revealing it; to refuse to give.

d) a formal accusation that initiates a criminal case.

e) to declare someone to be guilty of an offense during a trial at a court.

f) one's family or ethnic descent; the origin or a genetic line of descent.

g) the state of being enclosed within restricted boundaries as a prisoner, especially for political or military reasons.

Vocabulary Review

» Complete the following sentences with the words in the box. Words may be altered for grammatical necessity. Words may be used more than once.

> internment, ancestry, convict, vacate, uphold, withhold, indictment

- Jiho was accused of speeding and obstruction of justice. In court, he asserted that he was only pulled over because of his ___(a)___. He said he had overheard the police officers saying, "These people think they are special, so they drive like maniacs." After the prosecutor delivered his ___(b)___ at the trial, Jiho requested the audio recordings of the police officers' body cameras as evidence. Howverver, the police department ___(c)___ the recordings, asserting that they had lost all the bodycam recordings of that day in a flood. Failing to prove his innocence, Jiho was ___(d)___ at the trial court.

- Andrea failed to pay her rent because she was in an ___(e)___ camp in a foreign country. Her landlord filed for an eviction order that was granted by default judgment.* Andrea is going to file an appeal against the default judgment and establish a valid reason for not appearing in court in order to ___(f)___ the initial ruling.

* default judgment: a ruling granted by a judge or court in favor of a plaintiff in the event of that the defendant in a legal case fails to respond to a court summons or does not appear in court.

Watch the Video

» You will watch a video on a case related to a U.S. Supreme Court decision. While you are watching the video, focus on the questions in the table below and take notes to answer the questions.

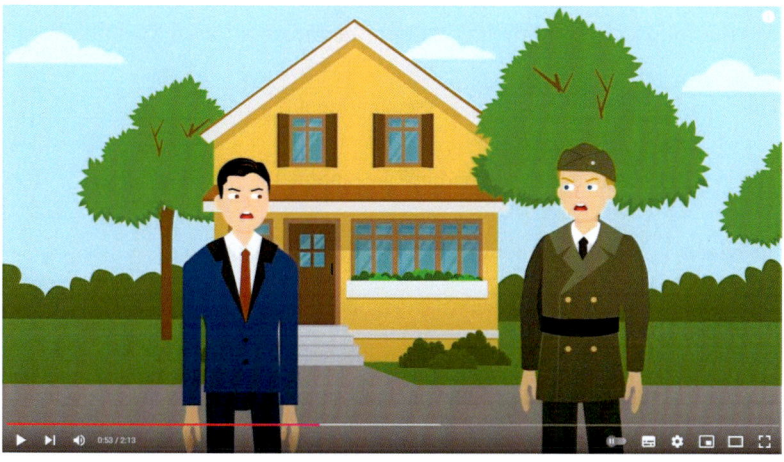

- Who is/are involved in the case?

- Whose interests are related?

- What is the main question in the case?

- Timeline

Listening Comprehension Quiz

» This time, only the audio will be played. Listen carefully and complete the quiz below to review what you learn.

• True/False/Not Given

How do the following statements relate to the information in the audio?

True	The audio verifies the statement.
False	The audio contradicts the statement.
Not Given	The statement cannot be verified by the audio.

Q1. According to the new law and policy, people in certain areas were not allowed to stay and were ordered to move to other places.

Q2. The government hid evidence favorable to Korematsu from the court.

Q3. When the government confronted Korematsu at a later trial, they admitted to their own mistakes.

• Multiple Choice

Q4. According to the audio, which of the following statement(s) *CANNOT* be verified?

a) Korematsu believed that the internment of Japanese Americans was unjust.
b) Additional threats to national security caused by Japanese were unproven.
c) After a long time after the war, Congress reexamined the military necessity of the internment.
d) The government would not admit their wrongdoings because they worried about the following law suits by many other Japanese.

Food for Thought

» Consider the video and your own experiences. Discuss the following questions with your partners.

- In what kind of situations is it acceptable to restrict the freedoms of others? To what extent can those freedoms be restricted? Are there types of freedom that may not be restricted?

- If you were the president or a member of Congress of the U.S. in 1942, what other options could have been pursued besides the internment of a certain ethnic group?

LESSON 4

READING KOREMATSU V. UNITED STATES (1944)

💬 Before Reading

The following image is a syllabus of the Korematsu case in 1944 at the United States Supreme Court. We examined a Supreme Court syllabus on p. 49 in Unit I. With your partners, discuss the questions below.

- Identify the petitioner and respondent.
- Is there anything that stands out to you?

SUPREME COURT OF THE UNITED STATES
323 U.S. 214
Korematsu v. United States
Argued: October 11, 12, 1944
Decided: December 18, 1944

Syllabus

1. Civilian Exclusion Order No. 34 which, during a state of war with Japan and as a protection against espionage and sabotage, was promulgated by the Commanding General of the Western Defense Command under authority of Executive Order No. 9066 and the Act of March 21, 1942, and which directed the exclusion after May 9, 1942, from a described West Coast military area of all persons of Japanese ancestry, *held* constitutional as of the time it was made and when the petitioner — an American citizen of Japanese descent whose home was in the described area — violated it. P. 219.

2. The provisions of other orders requiring persons of Japanese ancestry to report to assembly centers and providing for the detention of such persons in assembly and relocation centers were separate, and their validity is not in issue in this proceeding. P. 222. **[p215]**

3. Even though evacuation and detention in the assembly center were inseparable, the order under which the petitioner was convicted was nevertheless valid. P. 223.

CERTIORARI, 321 U.S. 760, to review the affirmance of a judgment of conviction.

MR. JUSTICE BLACK delivered the opinion of the Court.

Useful Words for Reading

» Confirm whether or not you are familiar with the words below. If you recognize the word, write the definition in the given box. Refer to the 'Hints' to discuss with your partners and guess the meanings of the words you don't know.

	Known/Unknown	Hint
comply		Sense of "to fulfill an order"
detention		Sense of "hold back"
evacuation		Sense of "to empty"
imperative		Sense of "must"
concur		Sense of "run together", "together with"
contend		Sense of "compete with"

» Check your previous knowledge of the following words on the left and match them to the definitions on the right.

- **comply** a) to be of the same opinion; to agree.

- **detention** b) to strive in debate; to dispute earnestly.

- **evacuation** c) to act or be in accordance with wishes, requests or demands; to meet specific standards.

- **imperative** d) something that demands attention or action; unavoidable obligation or requirement.

- **concur** e) removing persons or things from a place.

- **contend** f) maintenance of a person in custody or confinement, usually for a short period of time.

Vocabulary Review

» Complete the following sentences with the words below. Words may be altered for grammatical necessity.

- comply
- evacuation
- concur
- detention
- imperative
- contend

- There was a military encounter with a hostile country near the border during the presidential election campaign. It is necessary to implement a political ___(a)___ . Both political parties ___(b)___ with the ___(c)___ of civilians from the area and the postponing of election day.

- The public's attention was absorbed with the news that a famous sport star and her fiancé were arrested for killing a mom and 14-month-old infant in a stroller. The mom and baby died in a car accident caused by the two celebrities while under the influence of narcotics and alcohol. The couple ___(d)___ that they took legal medicine prescribed by a doctor and they didn't break any traffic laws. When the judge dismissed the warrant for the arrest of the offenders, the public was enraged. The trial court declared a suspension of execution to the couple claiming that the defendants are law-abiding citizens with secure jobs and residence. Since they are constantly monitored by the public, it makes them low flight risks. The court also said that the defendents have ___(e)___ with the court's order and have shown sincere regret. The court said it is hard to sentence the defendents to severe punishment like actual imprisonment. The public was outraged once again. People gathered in front of the court and began a protest. Unfortunately, it turned violent, and twelve protesters were arrested and tried at a summary trial and sentenced to 40 days' ___(f)___ .

Key Legal Terms for Reading

» The following concept is useful for reading the passages in this lesson. Read the passage below, and with your partners, discuss what you think is the main idea or key information is in the passage. You can circle or underline the phrases you think are important.

- **probation**

From its dictionary definition, we can easily assume the legal meaning of probation. Probation is a noun meaning "the act of testing" or "the testing or trial of a person's conduct, characteristics or qualification."

The legal meaning of probation refers to "the state of having been conditionally released." If placed under probation, convicts are sent back into the community instead of to prison and placed under the supervision of a probation officer.

Under the guidelines of the legal system, a judge can sentence an offender to jail time or probation after considering such aspects as the severity of the crime, whether or not the convict was a repeat offender, and the offender's status as a minor or not.

Mini Discussion!

Consider the dictionary definition of "probation" in the passage above. How do you think the meaning of the original phrase influences its legal meaning at court?

Reading Passage

» Read the following passage carefully and prepare to answer the questions in the reading comprehension quiz.

In response to the Japanese attack on Pearl Harbor during World War II, President Franklin Roosevelt signed Executive Order 9066 on February 1942. The order authorized the Secretary of War and the armed forces to remove people of Japanese ancestry from what they designated as military areas and surrounding communities in the United States and place them in relocation centers.

Fred Korematsu (23) was a Japanese-American citizen who did not comply with the order to leave his home and job. The FBI arrested Korematsu for failure to report to a relocation center. After his arrest, he decided to challenge the constitutionality of the government's order. The case was tried in federal court in San Francisco, and Korematsu was convicted of violating military orders issued under Executive Order 9066, given five years of probation, and sent to an Assembly Center in San Bruno, CA.

After the U.S. Court of Appeals upheld the trial court's decision asserting that he violated military order, he appealed the appellate decision to the Supreme Court of the United States. The central question of this case was whether or not the government went beyond its powers by implementing actions that resulted in the violation of the rights of Americans of Japanese descent.

On December 18, 1944, a divided Supreme Court ruled, in a 6-3 decision, that the detention was a "military necessity" not based on race. In an opinion written by Justice Black, the Court ruled that the evacuation order violated by Korematsu was valid since it did not show racial prejudice but rather responded to the strategic imperative of keeping the U.S. and particularly the West Coast (the region nearest Japan) secure from invasion. Justice Frankfurter concurred, writing that the "martial necessity arising from the danger of espionage and sabotage" warranted the military's evacuation order.

Continues on the next page ☞

Justice Jackson dissented, arguing that the exclusion order legitimized racism that violated the Equal Protection Clause of the Fourteenth Amendment. In his strongly worded dissent, Justice Robert Jackson contended that "Korematsu ... has been convicted of an act not commonly thought a crime." The nation's wartime security concerns, he continued, did not give adequate reason to strip Korematsu and the other internees of their constitutionally protected civil rights.

Adapted from
Justia Law. (2003). *Korematsu v. United States, 323 U.S. 214 (1944)*. https://supreme.justia.com/cases/federal/us/323/214/
Oyez Project. (1980). *Korematsu v. United States*. Oyez. https://www.oyez.org/cases/1940-1955/323us214

Reading Comprehension Quiz

» Check your understanding by answering the questions below.

• True/False/Not Given

How do the following statements relate to the given passage?

True	The passage verifies the statement.
False	The passage contradicts the statement.
Not Given	The statement cannot be verified by the passage.

Q1. The majority of justices believed that certain areas were especially vulnerable to Japanese military action and spies.

Q2. Korematsu was found guilty because he disguised himself to conceal his identity in order to avoid relocation and flee to Japan.

Q3. Due to his anti-social personality, Korematsu failed to comply with the military order.

Q4. A trial court judge interpreted Korematsu's violation of the relocation order as a serious offense that required monitoring for several years.

• **Summarizing**

Q5. Choose the best pair of words that could be placed in the blanks to complete the summary.

- After the U.S. was attacked by Japan, the government implemented a new policy of Japanese ____(X)____ from certain regions. Japanese American Fred Korematsu refused to relocate and was arrested by the authorities. In court, Korematsu questioned the constitutionality of the government's policy. The majority opinion of the Supreme Court found that the policy was constitutional because it did not aim to discriminate against a certain ethnic group. Instead, it was an ____(Y)____ that guaranteed national security. The dissent stressed that national security could not justify policies that were based on racial discrimination.

	X	Y
a)	internment	initiative
b)	exclusion	patriotism
c)	removal	imperative
d)	integration	strategy

Finding and Countering Logical Fallacies

» Do you agree with the reasoning of the majority opinion of the Supreme Court? With your partners, discuss what kind of logical fallacies might be relevant in the majority opinion and the concurring opinion in Korematsu 1944. Then, formulate your counter statements. You can refer to the sample of countering logical fallacies on p. 106 and the dissenting opinion by Justice Jackson.

- Step 1: Identify the error in reasoning.
- Step 2: Explain why it's not logical.
- Step 3: Provide a strong opposing contention and rationale. (Optional)

LESSON 5

READING KOREMATSU V. UNITED STATES (1984)

💬 Before you read

By watching the video and reading the U.S. Supreme Court precedent set in 1944, we learned what Fred Korematsu went through. Reminding yourself of what you learned from the previous lessons, take a look at the image of the court decision on the bottom. With your partners, find and circle answers to the questions below on the image of the court decision.

- Where was this decision made?
- Who are the parties of the case and how are they referred to?
- Who delivered the court opinion?
- Is there anything else that stands out to you?

---

584 F. Supp. 1406 (1984)

Fred KOREMATSU, Plaintiff,
v.
UNITED STATES of America, Defendant.

No. CR-27635 W.

United States District Court, N.D. California.

April 19, 1984.

*1407 *1408 *1409 William T. McGivern, Asst. U.S. Atty., San Francisco, Cal., Victor Stone, Counsel for Special & Appellate Matters, General Litigation & Legal Advice Section, U.S. Dept. of Justice, Washington, D.C., for defendant.

Dale Minami, Minami & Lew, San Francisco, Cal., Peter Irons, Leucadia, Cal., Robert L. Rusky, Hanson, Bridgett, Marcus, Vlahos & Stromberg, Ed Chen, Coblentz, Cahen, McCabe & Breyer, Eric Yamamoto, San Francisco, Cal., for plaintiff.

OPINION

PATEL, District Judge.

Fred Korematsu is a native born citizen of the United States. He is of Japanese ancestry. On September 8, 1942 he was convicted in this court of being in a place from which all persons of Japanese ancestry were excluded pursuant to Civilian

Useful Words for Reading

» Confirm whether or not you are familiar with the words below. If you recognize the word, write the definition in the given box. Refer to the "Hints" to discuss with your partners and guess the meanings of the words you don't know.

	Known/Unknown	Hint
pro bono		Regarding legal fees
suppress		Sense of "to put something down"
discount		Sense of "importance"
vigilant		Sense of "keep awake"
accountability		Sense of "responsibility"
remedy		As a noun or as a verb

» Check your previous knowledge of the following words on the left and match them to the definitions on the right.

- **pro bono** a) keenly watchful, carefully noticing problems or signs of danger.

- **suppress** b) a noun used in the legal context to refer to a method of enforcing a right or redressing a wrong; also, a verb that means "to cure" or "to correct."

- **discount** c) to leave out of an account; to disregard.

- **vigilant** d) (of legal work) without charge to the client.

- **accountability** e) to withhold from disclosure or publication.

- **remedy** f) the state of being reasonable and responsible.

Vocabulary Review

» Complete the following sentences with the appropriate words from the word box below. Words may be altered for grammatical necessity.

- pro bono
- discount
- accountability
- suppress
- vigilant
- remedy

- The uncle of a 14-year-old girl was on trial for negligence after the girl drowned while in his care. He claimed that he was free of ___(a)___ and not required to be ___(b)___ while caring for the girl, who was old enough to take care of herself. The court ruled that the uncle was guilty of negligence, stressing that the criminal conviction of the defendant does not provide a ___(c)___ for the parents, who had lost a child.

- The firm offered ___(d)___ services to the boys who were accused of armed robbery and the murder of an 82-year-old lady. The defendants asserted that they confessed to the crime during the police investigation because they faced physical violence. The defendants' attorneys requested a video recording of the interrogation, but the police ___(e)___ the evidence, testifying that the video recording system malfunctioned, and they could not access the recordings of the interrogation. The trial court judge decided to ___(f)___ the confession due to the fact that its validity could not be confirmed.

> **Key Legal Terms for Reading**

» The following concept is useful for this lesson. Read the passage below, and with your partners, discuss what you think is the main idea or key information in the passage. You can circle or underline the phrases you think are important.

• A Writ of Coram Nobis

The term *coram nobis* is an abbreviated Latin phrase meaning that "things remain in our presence." A writ of coram nobis is a legal order that allows a court to correct its original judgement upon discovery of a fundamental error that did not appear in the records of the original trial. A writ of coram nobis is applied only to criminal proceedings. A petition for a writ of *coram nobis* is not an appeal, but a request to seek a correction from the same court in which the original judgement was made.

Mini Discussion!

Consider the original meaning of the Latin phrase "coram nobis" in the passage above. How do you think the meaning of the original phrase influences its legal meaning at court?

Reading Passage

» Read the following passage carefully and prepare to answer the questions on the next page.

In 1983, a pro bono legal team with new evidence reopened the 40-year-old case of Korematsu v. United States in a federal district court on the basis of government misconduct. They showed that the government's legal team had intentionally suppressed or destroyed evidence from government intelligence agencies reporting that Japanese Americans posed no military threat to the U.S. The official reports, including those from the FBI, were not presented in court. On November 10, 1983, a federal judge overturned Korematsu's conviction in the same San Francisco courthouse where he had been convicted as a young man. The federal district court ruling cleared Korematsu's name, but the Supreme Court decision still stood.

Judge Patel delivered the district court's opinion, quoting the Supreme Court's opinion about coram nobis. A writ of coram nobis is a remedy by which the court can correct errors in criminal convictions. Judge Patel wrote that the Supreme Court has cautioned that coram nobis should be used "only under certain circumstances compelling such action to achieve justice" and to correct "errors of the most fundamental character." She believed that the Executive Branch and Congress were entitled to reasonably rely upon certain facts and to discount others, but the court also needed all the facts known by the government.

In this case, the government has taken a position equivalent to a confession of error without actually confessing to error. The government has eagerly moved to dismiss the case without acknowledging any specific reasons for dismissal. Under the U.S. legal system, a writ of coram nobis was used to correct errors of fact, so the court's decision did not remedy any errors of law suggested by Korematsu. Therefore, the Supreme Court's decision stood as the law of this case and for whatever precedential value it may still have.

In conclusion, Judge Patel stressed that Korematsu is important both as legal and political history. As historical precedent, it stands as a constant caution that in times of war or declared military necessity our institutions must be vigilant

Continues on the next page ☞

in times of war or declared military necessity our institutions must be vigilant in protecting constitutional guarantees. At the same time, the shield of military necessity and national security must not be used to protect governmental actions from close scrutiny and accountability. Therefore, Judge Patel ordered that a writ of coram nobis be granted and denied the counter-motion of the respondent.

Adapted from
Immigration History. (2019, September 27). *Korematsu v. United States (1984)*. https://immigrationhistory.org/item/korematsu-v-united-states-1984/
The Administrative Office of the U.S. Courts. (n.d.). *Facts and case summary - korematsu v. U.S.* https://www.uscourts.gov/educational-resources/educational-activities/facts-and-case-summary-korematsu-v-us

Reading Comprehension Quiz

» Check your understanding by answering the questions below.

• True/False/Not Given

How do the following statements relate to the given passage?

True	The passage verifies the statement.
False	The passage contradicts the statement.
Not Given	The statement cannot be verified by the passage.

Q1. Because of the exceptional conditions and for the purpose of pursuing justice, Judge Patel handed down a decision that is incompatible with the earlier Supreme Court's conclusion about Korematsu.

Q2. Judge Patel quoted a Supreme Court decision about Korematsu in 1944 which justified the power of coram nobis.

Q3. The defendant admitted misconduct but claimed that the case should not be tried.

Q4. Judge Patel established a new precedent that asserted that the government could not rely on the justification of national security in any case.

• **Summarizing**

Q5. Choose the best pair of words that could be placed in the blanks to complete the summary.

- Four decades after Korematsu was convicted, the federal district court ____(X)____ its former decision based on new evidence that was not submitted to the court at the original trial. In order to achieve justice and correct the error of the previous decision, the district court judge overturned Korematsu's previous guilty conviction. However, ____(Y)____ has power only over the fact of the case, so the Supreme Court decision and its reasoning about the constitutionality of the law that made Korematsu guilty in the past was still valid.

	X	Y
a)	contended	coram nobis
b)	remanded	pro bono
c)	vacated	pro bono
d)	overruled	coram nobis

Comparing the Two Precedents

» Referring to what you read in Lesson 4, compare the two different courts' decisions about the same party. Then, find information from the passage to answer the questions in the following chart.

Korematsu v. U.S. 1944	Korematsu v. U.S. 1984
• What values are competing each other?	• What values are competing each other?
• What is the main outcome of the decision?	• What is the main outcome of the decision?
• What are the reasons for the main outcome?	• What are the reasons for the main outcome?

vs

LESSON 6
MOCK TRIAL CASE ANALYSIS

💬 Roles and Responsibilities

In this lesson, you will analyze the case. Before we start, remind yourself of the roles of the participants in a mock trial. The following image shows a brief summary of each party's role and responsibilities.

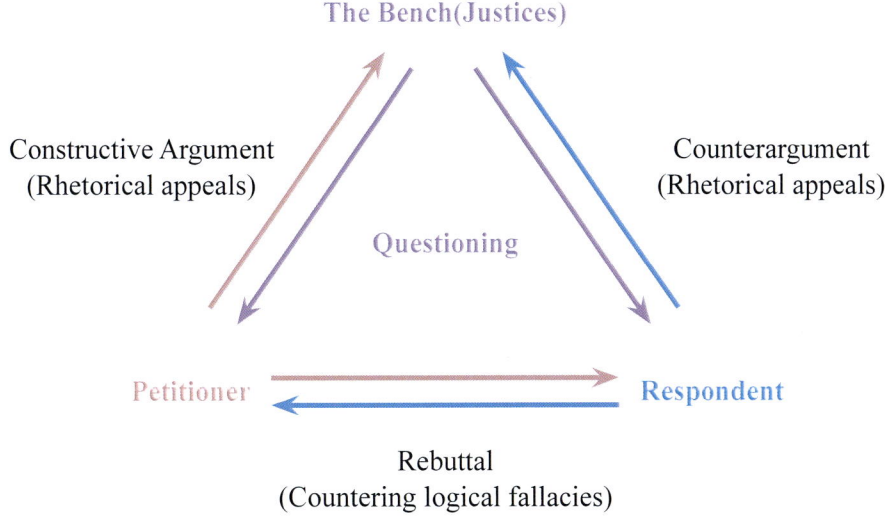

- A mock trial activity allows you to practice your debate skills using your knowledge of logical fallacies—in addition to rhetorical appeals—and oral arguments at a court setting.
- You will take care to consider both sides of the issue in order to build a stronger argument and employ counterarguments prepared in advance.

The Case

» The following passage provides the background and relevant details of the case that you will use for the mock trial activity. Read the passage and prepare yourself for the case analysis activities beginning on p. 138.

- **Background of the case**

17-year-old high school student Chani Shin is a citizen of the Republic of Chustia. Chani, who was born to a Chustian father and a Haponese mother, was raised in a provincial town in the Republic of Chustia and is attending Mirabilis Foreign Language High School. He is a 1st year student at MFL High, hoping to learn his mother's native language and eventually major in International Studies in college. MFL High is a special type of high school. Unlike general high schools, students choose one particular foreign language as their specialty and complete a curriculum aimed at developing a deep understanding of that language. As a Haponese-Chustian descendent who has Chustian nationality, Chani has a keen interest in issues regarding Chusita-Hapon relations including history.

During World War I, Chustia was colonized and annexed by Hapon until the end of World War II. During the occupation of Chustia by Hapon, Hapon prohibited Chustians from using the Chustian native language. Instead, Chustians were forced to learn and adopt Haponese as the official language. This was part of a policy aimed at expunging Chustian identity.

Chustia National University (CNU) was originally established during Haponese occupation as The Imperial University of Hapon (IUH) Chustia campus. After Chustia achieved independence from Hapon, and the Republic of Chustia was established, IUH Chustia campus was reopened as the current school Chustia National University (CNU), a public institution funded by the Chustia government. While CNU was IUH Chustia campus, Haponese was taught and studied in the Department of National Language and Literature, and Chustian was banned from being taught or studied. In order to effectively recover and develop the national and cultural identity of Chustia, CNU decided to teach the Chustian language and literature in the Department of National Language and Literature. Additionally, CNU did not establish a separate department to continue the study of the Haponese language and literature.

This year, CNU released a new admission plan for freshmen after conducting a year-long study and review of the current domestic laws on college education and college admission. According to the plan, admission will be decided based on an applicant's high school grade point average (GPA), scores on the National Exam for Secondary Education (NESE), and a college admission test designed by CNU specifically for CNU applicants. In particular, the applicant's high school GPA will be weighted 40%, the NESE will be weighted 20%, and CNU's college admission test will be weighted 40%. CNU's college admission test consists of four test subjects. There are three mandatory test subjects, which are Chustian Language and Literature, English and mathematics, and one elective subject among foreign languages. CNU released the updated list of five elective subjects including four foreign languages: Mandarin, French, German, Spanish, and Chinese characters and classics. This plan will be used for applicants who are currently in their 1st year in high school.

Chani believes that CNU's new admission plan is unfair to students like him since Haponese is not provided as an elective test subject. It means he needs to spend extra time and effort to learn and study a new language. This will impede his preparations for college admission to CNU and lower his chances of learning from the prestigious faculty in the Department of International Studies at CNU, Chani's long-term goal. In response to the new policy, Chani sued CNU at trial court, arguing that he has been discriminated against and treated unequally since the plan excludes Haponese from its test subjects.

- **Lower Court Decision**

The trial court ruled in favor of CNU, taking CNU's argument that Chani's suit does not merit challenging the legality of this admission plan. It is possible that he may experience a violation of his rights in the future when he applies for the

Continues on the next page ☞

test, but no violation has occurred at the moment of the trial. Additionally, since he still has at least one year to prepare for taking the test in another foreign language, it cannot be said that he was unequally treated. Moreover, since Haponese adopts Chinese Characters and Classics, broadly speaking, he can easily adjust his language of study to other test subjects like Chinese Characters and Classics. Chani appealed the trial court's decision. The Appellate Court of Chustia agreed with the trial court and affirmed its earlier decision. So he decided to appeal the decision to the Supreme Court of Chustia.

Adapted from
Constitutional Court of Korea. (2019). *Case on Seoul National University's Entrance Examination Plan, 92Hun-Ma68 (1992).* https://english.ccourt.go.kr/site/eng/decisions/casesearch/caseSearch.do

Case Analysis

» After reading the case brief carefully, with your partners, determine the parties and what kind of outcome they are seeking.

Petitioner	Respondent

» Read the case of Korematsu (1944) on pp. 123-124 in Lesson 4 again and compare Chani's case with Korematsu (1944). List their similarities and differences below.

Similarities	Differences
Example	Example
There is an instance of discrimination against a particular country.	*The Korematsu case is about ethnicity and Chani's is about language education.*

Law for the Case

» The following is the Law of the Republic of Chustia. Make references to the law in order to construct your argument in the mock trial.

- **The Constitution of the Republic of Chustia** (Excerpt)

    Article 9. The State shall strive to sustain and develop cultural heritage and to enhance national culture.

    Article 10. All citizens shall be assured of human worth and dignity and have the right to pursue happiness. It shall be the duty of the State to confirm and guarantee these fundamental and inviolable human rights.

    Article 11. All citizens shall be equal before the law, and there shall be no discrimination in political, economic, social, or cultural life on account of sex, religion, or social status.

    Article 22. All citizens shall enjoy freedom of learning and the arts.

    Article 31. All citizens shall have an equal right to receive an education corresponding to their abilities.

    Article 32. All schools and academic institutions shall enjoy freedom to work on educational programs to serve all citizens' freedom under this Constitution.

    Article 33. Independence, professionalism, political impartiality of education and the autonomy of institutions of higher learning shall be guaranteed under the conditions as prescribed by Act.

- **Elementary And Secondary Education Act** (Excerpt)

    Article 2 Types of Schools: The following schools shall be established to provide elementary and secondary education.

    1. Elementary schools

    2. Middle schools and civic high schools

    3. High schools and technical high schools

    4. Other various types of schools

- **Higher Education Act** (Excerpt)

Article 3 Classification of National School: Schools shall be classified into national schools established and managed by the State as national university corporations, public schools established and managed by local governments and private schools established and managed by incorporated school foundations.

Article 33 Qualifications for Admission: Those who have graduated from high schools or recognized as having equivalent or higher academic background under statutes or regulations are qualified to enter universities and colleges.

Article 34 Methods for Selecting Students:

(1) In selecting students to be admitted, the heads of universities or colleges shall endeavor to ensure that all people are guaranteed an equal right to education according to their abilities and that elementary and secondary education are provided in conformity with the original purposes of education.

(2) In conducting admission screening, the heads of universities or colleges shall prepare and implement various methods and standards to ensure temperament, aptitude, and abilities of students may be reflected.

Organizing Your Thoughts for Ethos

» Referring to Law

Law will be the main source cited in your rationale. With your partners, examine pp. 140-141 and discuss to determine what laws will be relevant to your argument.

Petitioner	Respondent
Example *The Constitution, Article 31* *: Petitioner shall have the opportunity to pursue an education corresponding to his ability so it is the state university's responsibility to make a college admission test corresponding to his foreign language proficiency.*	Example *The Constitution, Article 9* *: It is the state university's duty to enhance cultural heritage and culture. Given the school's limited resources, the school can exercise discretion in deciding which foreign language tests will be provided in line with promoting cultural heritage.*

Organizing Your Thoughts for Logos (1)

» Referring to Reasons

With your partners, discuss which of the following statements could be used in either parties' arguments. Write your own questions on the behalf of either party.

	Petitioner	Respondent
Does using Chinese characters make two different languages equivalent?	✓	
Is Haponese the only foreign language excluded from the language options?		
Is Chinese Characters and Classics a foreign language or one aspect of the Chustian language?		
Is the school capable of providing a Haponese language test?		
Can excluding Haponese from the range of test subjects be considered cultural xenophobia?		

C. Textbook 143

Organizing Your Thoughts for Logos (2)

» Refer to reasoning in Korematsu v. the United State

Even though the U.S. Supreme Court decision is not source of law applied in Chustia, it provides a reliable source of reasoning that could be used for comparison. Read the Korematsu cases in Lesson 4 and Lesson 5. Read your analysis on p. 134 again. Decide which Korematsu case can help the petitioner or the respondent. Quote the reasoning that you choose and write down how they are relevant in helping the petitioner or the respondent.

Petitioner	Respondent
Example	Example
A dissent of the Korematsu case in 19XX said "…."	*A dissent of the Korematsu case in 19XX said "…."*
(In dissenting opinion of the Korematsu case in 19XX " …..")	*(In dissenting opinion of the Korematsu case in 19XX " …..")*
or	*or*
The majority opinion in Korematsu 19XX said that……	*The majority opinion in Korematsu 19XX said that……*
(In majority opinion of the Korematsu case in 19XX " …..")	*(In majority opinion of the Korematsu case in 19XX " …..")*
or	*or*
Korematsu 19XX said that……	*Korematsu 19XX said that……*

Organizing Your Thoughts for Pathos

» With your partners, discuss how other factors can be used as appeals to pathos in your argument. You can exercise your creativity.

Petitioner	Respondent
Example *Petitioner is attending a special type of school and has spent more time and effort on studying Haponese compared to students who attend to regular high schools.*	Example *Chustia has experienced cultural genocide and being cut off from one's own language.*

LESSON 7

MOCK TRIAL PREP

💬 Selection of Counsels & Justices

As groups of 3~4, you will take the roles of the petitioner's counsel, respondent's counsel, and the justices on the bench.

1) Choose one person to be a team representative who will draw the role the team will adopt.
2) As a team of the petitioner's counsel or respondent's counsel, construct your argument together. Use the work for case analysis in Lesson 6 from pp. 138-145.
3) Each team will be given 15 minutes in total. Each counsel on your team will present at least once. Allot time properly between counsels and prepare arguments accordingly.
4) If you are assigned to the justices on the bench, decide who will play the role of Chief Justice and prepare possible questions for each constructive argument and counterargument.

» Case Info.: As discussed, complete the table below.

Official Reporter Citation	24 - 369
Caption of the Case	v.
Petitioner's Counsel	
Respondent's Counsel	
The Bench	Chief Justice Justices

Flow and Elements of Oral Argument

» The following image is a summary of the flow of the oral argument on p. 77 in the Unit I. Remember the elements of oral argument on p. 78 in the Unit I. In this unit, an additional element is required during rebuttal.

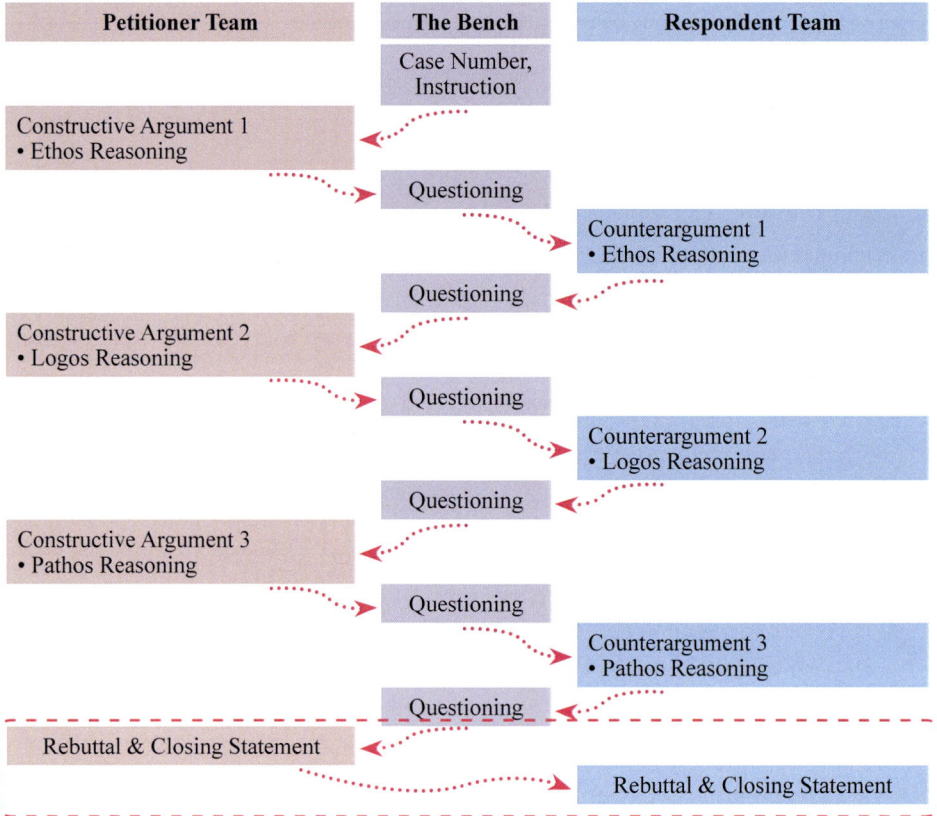

- Rebuttal

  A rebuttal means opposing the counterparty's argument using contrary proof. Exposing a logical fallacy in an opponent's argument is one way to present a rebuttal to their argument. During the rebuttal, you should try to include

  1) Counters to logical fallacies in the other party's oral argument or in the lower courts' decision.

  2) A recapitulation of the overall argument, an additional argument, and an answer to the counter of the logical fallacies.

Types of Questions by the Justices

» Remember the elements of questioning on p. 78 in Unit I. Questioning is a method by which the members of the bench communicate with not only the parties' counsels but also with their own colleagues on the bench. In this unit, questions by the justices need to be divided into two types.

1) Friendly questions
   - Rather easy type of questions which usually ask about the facts of the case.
   - A means of persuading the justice's colleagues toward a certain conclusion.[1]
   - A gracious tone and manner of questioning also helps to imply the justices' position toward the parties' arguments.
   - Since friendly questions are meant to bring out the strengths of a counsel's argument, counsel might want to pay attention to when these friendly questions are delivered and attempt to strengthen their arguments even more.

Mini Discussion!

In this context, what might "friendly" mean?

2) Merit testing questions
   - In law, merits refers to "inherent rights and wrongs of a legal case, absent of any emotional or technical bias."[2]
   - The goal of the merit test is to determine whether or not it is reasonable to accept the parties' argument.[3]
   - The merit test attempts to define any benefit that the party might expect to gain.

Mini Discussion!

Consider the dictionary meaning of "merit." How might it relate to its legal meaning?

---

[1] Brostoff, T. K., & Sinsheimer, A. (2013). *United States Legal Language and Culture: An Introduction to the U.S. common law system* (3rd ed.). p.199. Oceana.
[2] Wikimedia Foundation. (2023, May 6). *Merit (law)*. Wikipedia. https://en.wikipedia.org/wiki/Merit_(law)
[3] Legal Aid Bureau. (n.d.). *Taking the merits test*. Ministry of Law Singapore. https://lab.mlaw.gov.sg/legal-services/taking-the-merits-test/

- Sample dialogue

    The following is an adapted excerpt from the sample dialogue on pp. 80-83 in Unit I. When you read the sample dialogue, note what could signal the types of questions and how counsels react. Keep in mind that counsels' proper respect for the bench is as important as concrete logic and rhetorical appeals in oral arguments.

    1) Friendly questions

    Respondent Counsel

    Mr. Chief Justice, and members of the Court, and may it please the Court: my name is Kathy Young, representing respondent Drumptown, LTD. The petitioner misunderstands the central issue here. The central issue is whether or not Mr. Niederman and his pet—an alligator—violate the peaceful life of his neighbors. Article II of the Constitution guarantees all citizens a peaceful life. Letting a vicious animal—an alligator—stroll around common areas such as a swimming pool is indisputably violating other tenants' right to a peaceful life.

    Justice

    May I ask whether this has anything to do with the fact that alligators might attack people?

    Respondent Counsel

    Yes, your Honor (thank you for the question), **if I may,** there have been multiple incidents where tenants have observed the alligator displaying hunting behaviors. Therefore, the central issue is not the right to keep the pet, but how it endangers the lives of other tenants.

2) Merit testing question

Petitioner Counsel

Mr. Chief Justice, and may it please the Court: I am Sue J. Lee, appearing on behalf of petitioner Mr. Niederman. The central issue here is whether or not Drumptown can evict Mr. Niederman because of his pet. First, Mr. Niederman is not obligated to empty his condo. This is because Drumptown's eviction order violates Article XX of the Constitution. Article XX protects an individual's right to possess animals as mean of private guard. Since the alligator is being used to protect Mr. Niederman, it deserves to be protected under Article XX.

Justice

Excuse me, but how do you suggest that the alligator serves as the protection of Mr. Niederman?

Petitioner Counsel

With respect your Honor, the alligator does not have to be trained to attack strangers. The mere presence of the alligator serves as a deterrent the same way "Beware of Dog" signs deter possible criminals.

Justice

However, counsel, might it be the case that a dog and an alligator are extremely different in terms of the amount of fear they can elicit? Is it possible that Mr. Niederman's pet put other neighbors in fear and the amount of suffering of his neighbors might outweigh the value of the alligator as a crime deterrent?

Petitioner Counsel

Your Honor, surely, the neighbors' fears can simply be interpreted as a prejudice against alligators the same way that certain people believe that every wine lover is a drunk driver.

Writing a Script for an Oral Argument

» If you are on the petitioner or respondent teams…

- As a team, discuss ideas for contentions and reasonings.

- Then, divide into the roles of counsel i) who will take parts of oral argument incorporating ethos, logos, and pathos, and ii) who will take the rebuttal.

- Make sure all the team members are prepared to argue against the opposing view.
  1) Each team member writes at least one script for their section of the oral argument and share the outline of their section with all members.
  2) Fill out the table with your name as counsel and label it with your role and write a script.
  3) Use what you learned about case analyses in Lesson 6 and countering logical fallacies in Lesson 2. Remember to use the argument structure on p. 35.
  4) For writing a script, refer to the sample argument on pp. 80-83 and make sure to use key expressions presented on p. 79.
  5) Refer to the speech style check list on p. 84, and practice with your team members.

Counsel:	**(Constructive/Counter) Argument**

Preparing Critical Inquiries for Questioning

» If you are on the justice bench...

- Elect the chief justice. Then, discuss what kinds of ideas and thoughts will be critically questioned while each party's counsels are delivering their oral arguments. Use the space in the table and prepare a list of possible questions.

- Two types of questioning
  Prepare both "friendly questions" and "merit testing questions" from the perspective of critical inquiry.
  1) Each team member should prepare at least two questions for the oral argument. Share the list of questions with the members.
  2) Use what you learned on case analyses in Lesson 6 to make critical questions. Try to find ideas beyond what you worked on while analyzing the mock trial case on pp. 138-145.
  3) Refer to the sample oral argument on pp. 80-83 and make sure to use key expressions in the oral argument on p. 79.
  4) You can use what you learned about identifying and countering logical fallacies in Lesson 2 for designing "merit testing questions".
  5) During questioning, you can also request clarification about facts or a restatement of the argument.

Justice:	Possible Questions

LESSON 8

TAKE IN ACTION

💬 In-class Mock Trial

Courtroom seating layout

Arrange the classroom so that it reflects the U.S. Supreme Court courtroom seating layout.

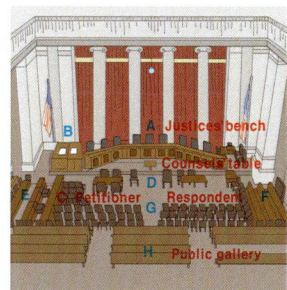 

» Instructions
  1) Take seats according to the Supreme Court courtroom layout.
  2) When the chief justice calls the case citation and caption, the trial begins. The chief justice informs each party that they have **12 minutes total for oral arguments** including answering the justices' questions. The chief justice informs the court that during the **3-minute rebuttal** at the end, each party can complete arguments that they haven't already finished.
  3) At each turn for the oral argument, counsels stand up at the center of counsel's table facing the justices at the bench.
  4) A camera and a screen will be placed behind the bench to show the counsel's argument to other counsels at the counsels' table.

In-class Mock Trial

» Recorder: During the oral argument, take notes, recording the other party's arguments and the justices' questions.

Petitioner's Argument
Constructive Argument 1

- Contention
- Reasons
- Supporting evidence/example
- Impact
- Logical fallacies (if any)
- Bench's questioning

Constructive Argument 2

- Contention
- Reasons
- Supporting evidence/example
- Impact
- Logical fallacies (if any)
- Bench's questioning

Constructive Argument 3

- Contention
- Reasons
- Supporting evidence/example
- Impact
- Logical fallacies (if any)
- Bench's questioning

Respondent's Argument
Counterargument 1

- Contention
- Reasons
- Supporting evidence/example
- Impact
- Logical fallacies (if any)
- Bench's questioning

Counterargument 2

- Contention
- Reasons
- Supporting evidence/example
- Impact
- Logical fallacies (if any)
- Bench's questioning

Counterargument 3

- Contention
- Reasons
- Supporting evidence/example
- Impact
- Logical fallacies (if any)
- Bench's questioning

Sample Syllabus

» A syllabus is a short summary of the legal basis of a court's decision. In a syllabus, the majority opinion of the court is presented.
» The following syllabus is an adapted version of the syllabus for the Fisher case. Refer to this sample when writing your own syllabus.

SUPREME COURT OF THE UNITED STATES	Court deciding the case
FISHER v. UNIVERSITY OF TEXAS AT AUSTIN	Caption of the case
No. 14-981. Argued December 9, 2015 - Decided June 23, 2016	Citation # Date
The University of Texas at Austin (University) uses an undergraduate admissions system… goal of providing the educational benefits of diversity to its undergraduate students. Petitioner Abigail Fisher, who was not in the top 10% was denied admission to the University's 2008 freshman class. She filed suit, alleging that the University's consideration of race… in violation of the Equal Protection Clause.	Summary of the case
Held: The race-conscious admissions program in use at the time of petitioner's application is lawful under the Equal Protection Clause.	Hold
(a) The laws and the Constitution protect citizens… and this supported what is addressed in evidence Fisher submitted to this court... Petitioner has not proved her point… (b) In Regent of University of California v. Bakke… (c) Even though the petitioner certainly gave a praiseworthy effort in her school works, the compelling interest of the state considers the struggles of minority groups as well as historical hardships and intangible elements that contribute to the court decision… For these reasons, the University's action did not violate the Equal Protection Clause.	Court's Legal Analysis
Kennedy, J., delivered the opinion of the Court, in which GINSBURG, BREYER, and SOTOMAYOR, JJ. joined.	Authoring Justices

Brainstorming and Outlining Your Own Syllabus

» Imagine your team's position is the majority opinion of the court. Refer to your work on pp. 138-145 in Lesson 6 and pp. 152-153 in Lesson 7. As a team, discuss how you might organize your ideas using the guiding questions below.

Summary of the case

- Who is the petitioner?

- What are the specifics of the case?

- What issue at stake? What is the petitioner alleging? What is the petitioner seeking?

Court's Legal Analysis

(a) Incorporate relevant laws and your analysis of the lower courts' decision.

(b) Include quotations from Korematsu.

(c) Evaluate the petitioner's appeals and the respondent's responses.

Writing a Syllabus

» Imagine that your team's position and argument is the majority opinion of the Court. Using your name as the authoring justice and your team members as the other justices, write a syllabus of your own.

SUPREME COURT OF CHUSTIA	Court deciding the case
v.	Caption of the case
No. 24-369. Argued , 20 - Decided , 20	Citation # Date
	Summary of the case
Held:	Hold

(a)   Court's
                                                                       Legal
                                                                       Analysis

(b)

(c)

For this reason,
                                                                       Authoring
                                                                       Justices

Personal Reflection

» In this unit, we examined cases involving cultural xenophobia that might illuminate the conflicts in our own society. Write your responses to the reflection questions below.

	Yes / No
Before this unit, did you feel that issues of xenophobia related to your real life problems?	
If yes, please explain what it was.	
If no, why not?	
Did you learn something new about xenophobia from this unit?	
If yes, please explain what you learned.	
After completing the entire unit, has your position or attitude toward xenophobia issues in our own society changed?	
Based on what you learned in this unit, what would you like to change in our society?	

D

Appendices

APPENDIX A

SCRIPT
UNIT I LESSON 3 p. 45

Fisher v. University of Texas (Fisher II) Case Brief Summary

» https://www.youtube.com/watch?v=e6J1GNXzh-o

It's fascinating to compare the Supreme Court's approach to affirmative action in two decisions arising out of the same case. We can consider Fisher versus University of Texas at Austin known as Fisher II.

The state of Texas enacted a Top Ten Percent Law, which guaranteed the top 10 percent of every Texas high school graduating class admission to any Texas public university. The University of Texas admitted applicants who qualified under the law, then filled out its incoming freshman class using a combination of academic and college admissions test scores, as well as what it called a Personal Achievement Index. The index was based on a holistic review and considered an applicant's extracurricular work, community and leadership record, home and socioeconomic factors, and the applicant's race, favoring African American and Hispanic applicants.

Abigail Fisher unsuccessfully applied for admission to the university in 2008. Fisher wasn't in the top 10 percent of her class, so was evaluated based on her academic and index scores. Fisher then sued, alleging that the university's consideration of race violated the equal protection rights of Caucasian applicants. The district court held the for the university and the Fifth Circuit affirmed. The United States Supreme Court then held that the use of race in university admissions decisions must withstand strict scrutiny. On remand the Fifth Circuit which again ruled for the university and again the Supreme Court granted cert.

APPENDIX A
SCRIPT
UNIT II LESSON 3 p. 115

Korematsu v. United States Case Brief Summary

» https://www.youtube.com/watch?v=5O8Xsda2AXk

Fred Korematsu was best known as the Japanese American who unsuccessfully challenged the constitutionality of the internment of Japanese Americans during World War II. Forty years after the United States Supreme Court decided his case, another court revisited the U.S. government's treatment of Korematsu in Korematsu v. United States.

In 1941, the U. S. declared war on Japan. The president issued Executive Order 9066 which gave the Secretary of War the power to designate military zones and keep people out of those areas. Congress made it a crime to ignore an order to leave a military zone. A portion of the West Coast was designated Military Area Number One. Then, an order excluded those of Japanese ancestry from living there unless they were in assembly centers. Fred Korematsu's ancestors were Japanese. He lived in Zone One but didn't report to an assembly center. Korematsu was convicted of breaking federal law, which was upheld on appeal.

Decades after the internment of Japanese Americans ended, Congress created The Commission on Wartime Relocation and Internment of Civilians. The commission's report stated that there wasn't a military necessity for internment. According to the report, the internment was an unjust product of racial prejudice, war hysteria, and leadership failures.

Korematsu filed a petition for a writ of coram nobis to vacate his conviction, arguing that the conviction resulted from the government's misconduct. In support, Korematsu cited the report and government memorandums showing the government withheld evidence that internment wasn't necessary from the courts. The U.S. responded. Though the government didn't admit to wrongdoing or specifically oppose the petition, it moved the court to vacate Korematsu's conviction and dismiss the indictment. The judge decided Korematsu's petition and the government's motion to vacate.

APPENDIX B

ANSWER KEYS
UNIT I

Lesson 1 Review the Concepts   p. 29

- (a) equality
- (b) equity
- (c) affiliation
- (d) disaffiliation
- (e) homogeneity
- (f) minority
- (g) majority
- (h) (i) race, gender

Lesson 2 Three Modes of Persuasion   p. 34

» The following are suggested answers. Please remember that some words might be used in different ways.

Logos	Ethos	Pathos
• statistics(interpretation of statistics) • facts (interpretation of facts) • law (when used as a source of reasoning. Ex: "The law requires that schools feed kids healthy food. Thus, we should give them more vegetables.") • reliable sources • experiments • survey results • test scores	• statistics (referring to the expertise of the one who compiled the statistics) • credibility • expert testimony • law (when used as a source of authority. Ex: "The law says the island is our sovereign territory, so that must be true.") • certificates • survey results (if relying on its authority) • anecdotes (if relying on the authority of the speaker)	• guilt • love • fairness • lust • self-esteem • pity • belief in fairness • revenge • trustworthiness (if appealing to the emotional aspect of being trustworthy. Ex: "We can trust Joe because he has always helped stray cats find their way home.")

• analogy • scientific evidence	• trustworthiness (if appealing to one's character or authority. Ex: "We should believe what Glenn has to say because he's a very trustworthy guy.")

Lesson 2 Analyzing a Sample Argument   p. 35

• **Sample**

The death penalty should be abolished in Korea. → **Contention**
First of all, it does not always effectively ensure justice. The death penalty is irreversible even if new evidence or judicial misconduct is discovered. Thus, → **Reason(Logos)**
innocent people may be sentenced to death. Secondly, the death penalty is inhumane since the right of → **Reason(Pathos)**
life is the essential to one's dignity. Lastly, the global stance towards the death penalty is rapidly changing. → **Reason(Ethos)**
By the end of 2021, two-thirds of nations in the world had abolished the death penalty. Abolishing the death → **Impact**
penalty is one way Korea can demonstrate its dedication to global efforts to protect human rights.

Lesson 3 Useful Words for Watching the Video   p. 42

» Matching meanings
• hold – (b), (d)   • affirm – (a), (c)

Lesson 3 Useful Words for Watching the Video   p. 43

» Matching meanings
• allege – (c)   • cert – (d)   • holistic – (e)
• index – (b)   • remand – (a)

» Completing sentences
- (a) alleged
- (b) held
- (c) remanded
- (d) affirmed

Lesson 3 Listening Comprehension Quiz   p. 46

» Listening comprehension quiz

• True/ False/ Not Given
Q1. True   Q2. Not Given   Q3. True

• Multiple Choice
Q4. (d)

Lesson 4 Useful Words for Reading   p. 50

» Matching meanings
- amendment – (c)
- appellate – (a)
- tailored – (b)

» Completing Sentences
- (a) amendment
- (b) tailored
- (c) appellate

Lesson 4 Key Legal Terms for Reading   p. 51

- Fourteenth Amendment   'additions',
                              'to protect individual rights and liberties.'

- Equal Protection Clause   'treat an individual in the same manners as others in similar conditions.'
                              'fair and equal treatment'

Lesson 4 Reading Comprehension Quiz   p. 53

» Reading comprehension quiz

• True/ False/ Not Given
Q1. False   Q2. True   Q3. True   Q4. Not Given

• Summarizing
(a) race   (b) equal protection   (c) Strict scrutiny

Lesson 5 Useful Words for Reading   p. 56

» Matching meanings

- feasibly - (d)
- compelling - (e)
- amorphous - (f)
- dissent - (c)
- deferential - (a)
- demographic - (b)

» Matching meanings in legal contents and in ordinary contents

- precedent – (b), (e)
- enact – (a), (c), (d)

Lesson 5 Vocabulary Review   p. 57

- Text 1.   (a) feasibly   (c) dissent   (e) deferential
            (b) demographic   (d) compelling
- Text 2.   (f) enacted   (g) precedent
- Text 3.   (h) precedent   (i) dissent   (j) enacted

Lesson 5 Analyzing the argument   p. 60

» the 1st paragraph, the majority opinion

The University of Texas' use of race as a consideration in the admission process did not violate the Equal Protection Clause of the Fourteenth Amendment. Justice Anthony M. Kennedy delivered the opinion for the 4-3 majority. The Court held that the University of Texas' use of race as a factor in the holistic review used to fill the spots remaining after the Top Ten Percent Plan was narrowly tailored to serve a compelling state interest. Previous precedent had established that educational diversity is a compelling interest as long as it is expressed as a concrete and precise goal that is neither a quota of minority students nor an amorphous idea of diversity. In this case, the Court determined that the University of Texas sufficiently expressed a series of concrete goals along with a reasoned explanation for its decision to pursue these goals along with a thoughtful consideration of why previous attempts to achieve the goals had not been successful. The University of Texas' Plan is

[Contention]
[Rationale / Ethos]
[Application to the case]

170 Think Like Lawyers, Speak Like Lawyers

also narrowly tailored to serve this compelling interest because there are no other available and workable alternatives for doing so. — Impact

» the 2nd paragraph, the second disssent

Justice Clarence Thomas wrote a dissent in which he argued that the Equal Protection Clause of the Fourteenth Amendment categorically prohibits the use of race as a consideration in higher education admissions process. In a separate dissent, Justice Samuel A. Alito Jr. wrote that the majority decision was too deferential to the University of Texas' determination that its use of race in the admissions process was narrowly tailored to serve compelling interest and that the majority failed to properly apply strict scrutiny. — Contention of Alito

Because the Fourteenth Amendment's Equal Protection Clause was enacted at least in part to prevent the government from treating individuals as merely components of racial class, race-based classifications, regardless of their purpose, must be subject to the strictest level of constitutional scrutiny. — Rationale 1 Logos

In this case, the University of Texas' use of race in its admissions policy cannot withstand strict scrutiny because the University's interest is not sufficiently and clearly defined and therefore judicial review to determine whether the policy is narrowly tailored is impossible. — Application to the case

Even if it were, the goal of demographic diversity could only feasibly be achieved using impermissible quotas for racial balancing that are based on stereotypes.

Justice Alito also argued that the use of racial preferences is unnecessary to achieve the goal of diversity because the admissions process could use a race- neutral holistic review based on life experiences that would achieve the same effect. — Rationale 2 Logos

Chief John G. Roberts, Jr. and Justice Clarence Thomas joined in the dissent.

Lesson 5 Reading Comprehension Quiz   pp. 61-62

» Reading comprehension quiz

• **True/ False/ Not Given**

Q1. True   Q2. False   Q3. Not Given   Q4. True

• **Summarizing**

Q5. (d)

APPENDIX B

ANSWER KEYS
UNIT II

Lesson 1 Review the Concepts   p. 99

- Text 1.   (a) nationalism   (b) patriotism
- Text 2.   (c) antagonism   (d) xenophobia   (e) prejudice
- Text 3.   (f) tolerance
- Tetx 4.   (g) segregation   (h) integration

Lesson 2 Identifying Logical Fallacies   p. 105

- (a) Hasty generalization
- (b) Straw man
- (c) Ad hominem (personal attack)
- (d) False cause (Post Hoc)
- (e) False comparison (faulty analogy)
- (f) Appeal to emotion
- (g) Ad populum (Bandwagon)
- (h) Red herring (diversion)

Lesson 3 Useful Words for Watching the Video   p. 113

» Matching meanings
- internment – (g)
- ancestry – (f)
- convict – (e)
- vacate – (b)
- uphold – (a)
- withhold – (c)
- indictment – (d)

Lesson 3 Vocabulary Review   p. 114

» Completing sentences

- Text 1.   (a) ancestry   (b) indictment   (c) withheld   (d) convicted
- Text 2.   (e) internment   (f) vacate

Lesson 3 Listening Comprehension Quiz   p. 116

» Listening comprehension quiz

• **True/ False/ Not Given**

Q1. True   Q2. True   Q3. False

• **Multiple Choice**

Q4. (d)

Lesson 4 Useful Words for Reading   p. 120

» Matching meanings

- comply – (c)   • detention – (f)   • evacuation – (e)
- imperative – (d)   • concur – (a)   • contend – (b)

Lesson 4 Vocabulary Review   p. 121

» Completing Sentences

- Text 1.   (a) imperative   (b) concur/concurred   (c) evacuation
- Text 2.   (d) contended   (e) complied   (f) detention

Lesson 4 Reading Comprehension Quiz   pp. 124-125

» Reading comprehension quiz

• **True/ False/ Not Given**

Q1. True   Q2. False   Q3. Not Given   Q4. True

• **Summarizing**

Q5. (c)

Lesson 5 Useful Words for Reading   p. 128

» Matching meanings

- pro bono – (d)
- suppress – (e)
- discount – (c)
- vigilant – (a)
- accountability – (f)
- remedy – (b)

Lesson 5 Vocabulary Review   p. 129

» Completing Sentences

- Text 1.   (a) accountability   (b) vigilant   (c) remedy
- Text 2.   (d) pro bono   (e) suppressed   (f) discount

Lesson 5 Reading Comprehension Quiz   pp. 132-133

» Reading comprehension quiz

• True/ False/ Not Given

Q1. True   Q2. False   Q3. False   Q4. False

• Summarizing

Q5. (d)

E
Teacher's Manual

Unit I Lesson 1

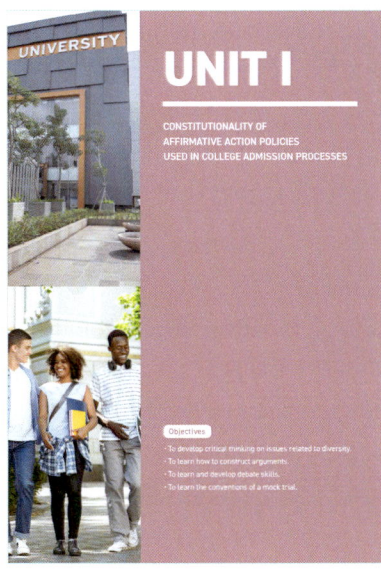

Suggested Times   ⏱ 8 minutes / p. 24

Aims
- To introduce the objectives and theme.
- To figure out students' familiarity with the theme.
- To activate students' schema.

Procedure/Instructions
1. Ask students to read the title and objectives.
2. Question students about unknown words in the title.
3. Provide the meanings of "constitutionality", "affirmative action policy", and "mock trial".
4. Ask students to recall their college admission experience and to guess how those words could be relevant to college admissions policies.

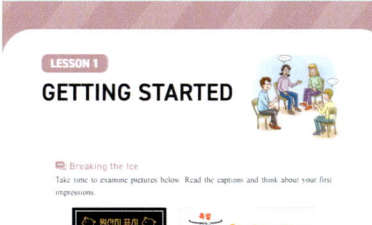

Suggested Times   ⏱ 6 minutes / p. 25

Aims
- To provide an opportunity to analyze code.
- To let students practice intensive reading.

Procedure/Instructions
1. Ask students to take a look at the pictures first and ask them if they have actually encountered something similar in their real lives.
2. Give 2 minutes to read the written description about the picture silently.
3. Give another 3 minutes to examine the pictures and think about whether or not they feel the pictures are problematic.

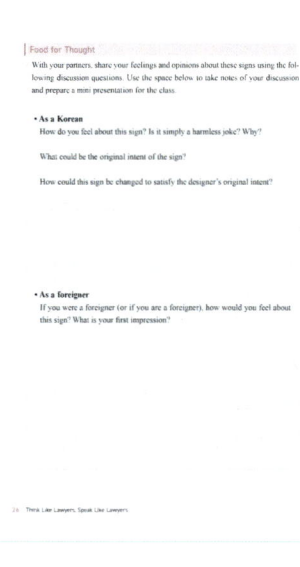

Suggested Times ⏱ 18 minutes / p. 26

Aims
- To provide opportunities to interpret potential problematic situations relevant to students' real lives.
- To let students practice interactive listening and speaking as well as writing skills for taking notes.

Procedure/Instructions
1. Give 1 minute to read the instructions and the discussion questions in the box.
2. Have students get into pairs or groups of three.
3. Give 10 minutes for discussion and 7 minutes to share their discussion with the class.

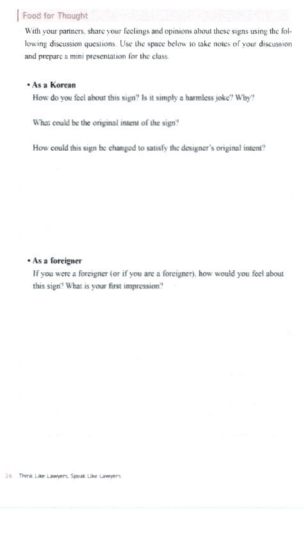

Suggested Times ⏱ 7 minutes / p. 27

Aims
- To introduce key concepts relevant to the theme of the unit and the topics in following lessons.
- To help students conceptualize words by analyzing code.

Procedure/Instructions
1. Tell students to work on this activity individually.
2. Ask students to read the instructions and words in the box carefully.
3. Ask students to take time to think about the pictures when they answer the questions.

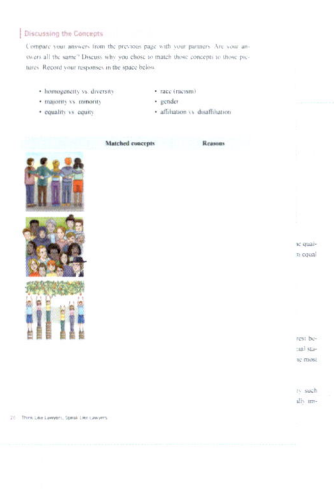

Suggested Times ⏱ 18 minutes / pp. 28-29

Aims

- To provide an opportunity to examine how others interpret the same thing differently.
- To let students practice interactive listening and speaking as well as writing skills for taking notes.
- To check students' understanding.

Procedure/Instructions

1. Have students get into pairs or groups of three.
2. Give 8 minutes to discuss the concepts.
3. Have 4 minutes to share the group discussion.
4. Give 3 minutes to solve the questions for reviewing the concepts.
5. Have 3 minutes to check answers and Q&A time.

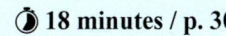

Suggested Times ⏱ 18 minutes / p. 30

Aims

- To provide opportunities to interpret critical potential problematic situations relevant to students' real lives.
- To let students practice interactive listening and speaking for discussion as well as writing skills for taking notes.

Procedure/Instructions

1. Give 1 minute to read the instructions and the discussion questions in the box.
2. Have students get into pairs or groups of three.
3. Give 12 minutes for discussion and 5 minutes to share their discussion with the class.

Unit I Lesson 2

Suggested Times 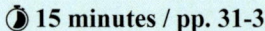 **15 minutes / pp. 31-32**

Aims

- To check students' general understanding about debate.
- To distinguish being good at debate versus winning at debate.
- To let students practice interactive listening and speaking for discussion as well as writing skills for taking notes.

Procedure/Instructions

1. Give 1 minute to take a look at and guess what is represented in the images.
2. Have students get into pairs or groups of three.
3. Give 10 minutes for discussion.
4. Give 4 minutes to share their group discussion with the class and have Q&A time.

Suggested Times 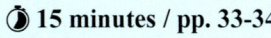 15 minutes / pp. 33-34

Aims
- To teach three modes of persuasion in rhetorical appeals.
- To check students' understanding.

Procedure/Instructions
1. Ask students if they know about Aristotle and give a chance to share their general knowledge about Aristotle. (2 minutes)
2. Bring students' attention to rhetorical appeals and read the description of logos, ethos, and pathos on p. 33. (1 minute)
3. Ask students if they need more explanation and ask them to move on to the next page and read the descriptions underneath logos, ethos, pathos in the table.
4. Have students get into pairs or groups of three and solve the task as they read the instructions at the top of the page. (12 minutes)

Suggested Times 7 minutes / p. 35

Aims
- To teach the structure and elements of argument.
- To provide an opportunity to distinguish the structure and the elements of argument in a sample.

Procedure/Instructions
1. Give 2 minutes to read the table of the elements of argument.
2. Ask students if there are difficult concepts and if they can distinguish rationale and reasons.
3. Give 3 minutes to do the task of analyzing a sample argument.

Suggested Times ⏱ **28 minutes / pp.36-38**

Aims

- To provide an opportunity to use the three modes of persuasion in students' own written arguments.
- To let students engage in teamwork for brainstorming.
- To let students practice writing an argument independently.

Procedure/Instructions

1. Tell students to work in teams to generate ideas and then work independently for writing an argument.
2. Explain the table on p. 36 where each color stands for a certain position and reasons for the position.
3. Make sure students try to think creatively when formulating supporting ideas and evidence for the reasons.
4. Give 13 minutes to work together on the task on p. 37.
5. Give 12 minutes to construct a written argument on p. 38 individually.

Suggested Times 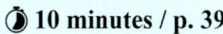 10 minutes / p. 39

Aims
- To let students practice analyzing written arguments.
- To provide opportunities to learn from classmates' work.

Procedure/Instructions
1. Ask students to exchange their written arguments with classmates whom they did not work together with for previous activities in the lesson.
2. Make sure students write constructive feedback for the additional comments and suggestions.
3. During the last 3 minutes, ask volunteers to share their overall reflection during peer reviewing.

Unit I Lesson 3

Suggested Times 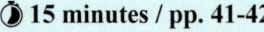 15 minutes / pp. 41-42

Aims
- To activate schema.
- To teach students that the meaning of a compound word might not necessarily be the sum of meanings and properties of the components in the compound word.
- To let students practice interactive listening and speaking as well as writing skills for taking notes.

Procedure/Instructions
1. Give 2 minutes to remind oneself of one's understanding about the meaning of "affirmative action".
2. Give 3 minutes to discuss the compound word, "affirmative action" as a pair or a group of three.
3. Give 10 minutes for further discussion.

Suggested Times 15 minutes / pp. 42-43

Aims
- To introduce useful vocabulary.
- To let students distinguish differences in meaning according to context.

Procedure/Instructions
1. Tell students to work on the first task on p. 42 as a pair or group of three.
2. Give 6 minutes to discuss the first task on p. 42.
3. Give 7 minutes to solve the rest 3 tasks up to p. 43 individually.
4. Check the answers together as a class and have Q&A time.

Suggested Times ⏱ 10 minutes / p. 44

Aims
- To provide background knowledge before watching a video.
- To teach legal terms useful for watching the video.
- To let students practice intensive reading to understand the meanings of central properties in compound words.

Procedure/Instructions
1. Give 2 minutes to read the passages individually.
2. Give 6 minutes for discussion as a pair or a group of three.
3. Share the answers as a class.

Suggested Times ⏱ 15 minutes / pp. 45-46

Aims
- To let students practice intensive listening as well as writing skills for taking notes.
- To provide an opportunity to build up schema for reading activities that students will work on in Lesson 4 and Lesson 5.

Procedure/Instructions
1. Tell students to work on this activity individually.
2. Before watching the video, let students go over questions in the table on p. 45.
3. Play the video for the tasks on p. 45. (3 minutes)
4. Play only the audio for the listening comprehension quiz on p. 46. (10 minutes)
5. Check the answers as a class and have Q&A.

E. Teacher's Manual 187

Suggested Times   ⏱ **20 minutes / p. 47**

Aims
- To provide opportunities to practice critical thinking about the topic in the video.
- To let students practice interactive listening and speaking as well as writing skills for taking notes.

Procedure/Instructions
1. Have students get into pairs or groups of three.
2. Ask students to recall their personal experiences of college admission.
3. Remind students to take notes of discussion.
4. Allot 15 minutes for group discussion and 5 minutes to share with the class.

Unit I Lesson 4

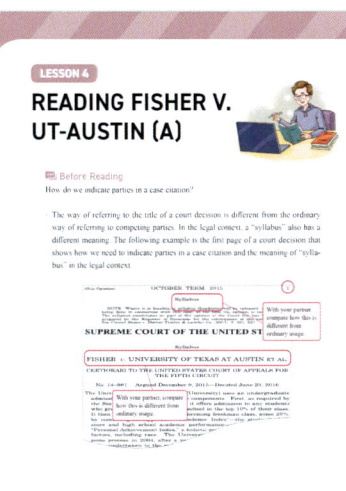

Suggested Times ⏱ 5 minutes / p. 49

Aims
- To let students distinguish different styles and different meanings according to the context.
- To let students practice interactive listening and speaking as well as wrting skills for taking notes.

Procedure/Instructions
1. Have students get into pairs or groups of three.
2. Give 3 minutes to read the instruction, examine the image, and share answers for the task within their groups.
3. Check the answers as a class and see if everyone agrees with the answers.

Suggested Times ⏱ 20 minutes / pp. 50-51

Aims
- To introduce useful vocabulary and key legal terms for reading.
- To prepare students to understand main idea of the reading passage.
- To let students practice intensive reading as well as interactive listening and speaking.

Procedure/Instructions
1. Tell students that they will work on the tasks on p. 50 individually and work as pairs or a groups of three for the task on p. 51.
2. Give 10 minutes for the tasks on p. 50.
3. Give 5 minutes for the tasks on p. 51.
4. Give 5 minutes to share the answers for the task on p. 51.

Suggested Times   ⏱ 25 minutes / p. 52

Aims

- To let students practice intensive reading.
- To prepare students for the mock trial activity that students will work on from Lesson 6 to Lesson 8.

Procedure/Instructions

1. Tell students to work on this task individually.
2. Give 10 minutes maximum to do silent reading for the reading passage on p. 52. Students who finish the reading earlier can move on to the reading comprehension quiz on p. 53.
3. Give another 8 minutes to solve the reading comprehension quiz. Students can refer to the reading passage.
4. Have 7 minutes to check answers as a class and to have Q&A time.

Suggested Times   ⏱ 25 minutes / p. 54

Aims

- To expand students' attention to topics that could be relevant to the main idea of the reading passage.
- To provide an opportunity to question the status quos that students observe in their real lives.
- To let students to practice interactive listening and speaking as well as writing skills for taking notes.

Procedure/Instructions

1. Have students get into pairs or groups of three.
2. Give 15 minutes for discussion.
3. Give 10 minutes to share the discussion to the class.

Unit I Lesson 5

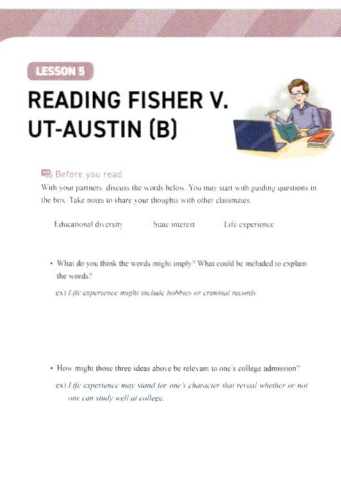

Suggested Times ⏱ 10 minute / p. 55

Aims
- To familiarize students with the crucial ideas in the upcoming reading activity.
- To provide opportunities to practice critical thinking.
- To let students practice interactive listening and speaking for discussion as well as writing skills for taking notes.

Procedure/Instructions
1. Have students get into pairs or groups of three.
2. Give 8 minutes for discussion.
3. Give 2 minutes to share their discussion with the class.

Suggested Times ⏱ 15 minutes / pp. 56-57

Aims
- To introduce useful vocabulary.
- To help students distinguish vocabulary differences according to context.

Procedure/Instructions
1. Tell students that they will work on the first task on p. 56 in pairs or groups of three, and work individually on the rest of the tasks up to p 57.
2. Give 10 minutes to solve the tasks.
3. Have 5 minutes to check answers as a class and to have Q&A time.

E. Teacher's Manual 191

Suggested Times ⏱ **10 minutes / pp. 58-59**

Aims

- To let students practice intensive reading.
- To provide an opportunity to build up schema to learn knowledge for composing a rationale for the mock trial activity in the upcoming lessons.

Procedure/Instructions

1. Tell students to work on this task individually.
2. Give 10 minutes maximum to do silent reading for the reading passage on pp. 58-59. Students who finish reading earlier can move on to work on the tasks from p. 59.

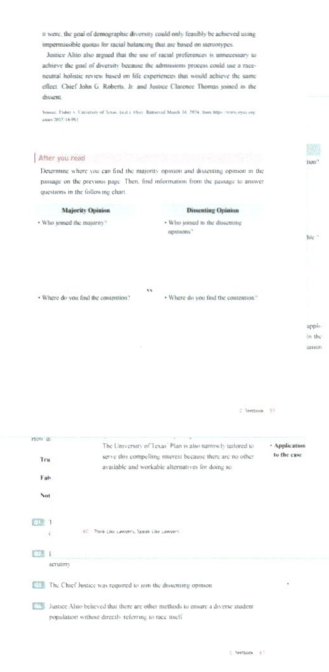

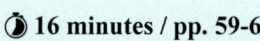

Suggested Times ⏱ **16 minutes / pp. 59-61**

Aims

- To analyze the text by comparing the majority opinion to the dissenting opinion.
- To provide opportunities to explore how each opinion constructs arguments and what critical ideas are used as reasons.

Procedure/Instructions

1. Tell students that they can work the tasks individually or in pairs.
2. Tell students that they can refer to the reading passage while they are working on the tasks.
3. Give 5 minutes to solve the task on pp. 59-60. Have 2 minutes to check answers as a class and have Q&A.
4. Give another 4 minutes to solve the second task on p. 60 and 2 minutes to check answers as a class and have Q&A.
5. Give 2 minutes to solve the first task on p. 61 and have 1 minute to check answers as a class and have Q&A.

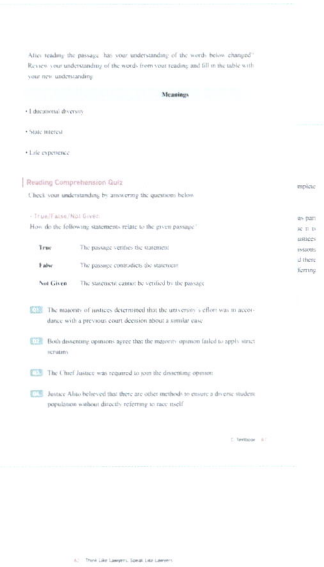

Suggested Times ⏱ 8 minutes / pp. 61-62

Aims
• To check students' understanding.

Procedure/Instructions
1. Tell students to work on this task individually.
2. Give 6 minutes maximum to solve the quiz. Students can refer to the reading passage.
3. Have 2 minutes to check answers as a class and to have Q&A time.

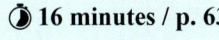

Suggested Times ⏱ 16 minutes / p. 63

Aims
• To introduce students to topics that might be relevant to the main idea of the reading passage.
• To provide the opportunity to question status quos that students observe in their real lives.
• To let students practice interactive listening and speaking for discussion as well as writing skills for taking notes.

Procedure/Instructions
1. Have students get into pairs or groups of three.
2. Give 10 minutes for discussion.
3. Give 6 minutes to share the discussion with the class.

Unit I Lesson 6

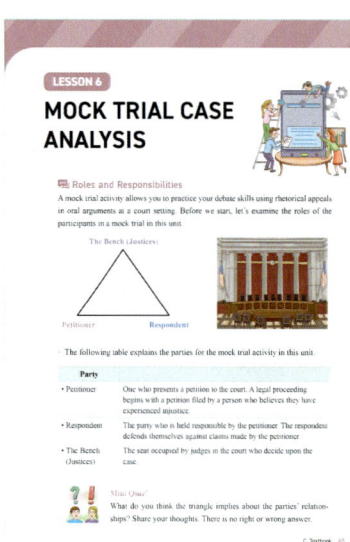

Suggested Times ⏱ 3 minutes / p. 65

Aims
- To introduce the purpose of the mock trial activity.
- To introduce students' roles and responsibilities in the upcoming activity.

Procedure/Instructions
1. Give 2 minutes to examine the diagram of the relationships between parties and the description of the roles in the table.
2. Discuss the mini quiz briefly.

Tip: During the mini quiz discussion, urge students to meditate on the concepts of fair competition and equal contribution.

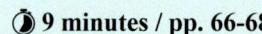

Suggested Times ⏱ 9 minutes / pp. 66-68

Aims
- To introduce the case for the mock trial activity.
- To let students practice skimming as an intensive reading skill.

Procedure/Instructions
1. Ask students to skim through the case silently and individually.
2. While students read the case, walk around and monitor in the event students have trouble understanding the case.
3. As a class, conduct a Q&A about the reading on the case.
4. Tell students they will return to the case during upcoming activities.

194 Think Like Lawyers, Speak Like Lawyers

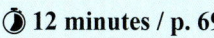

Suggested Times　　　⏱ **12 minutes / p. 69**

Aims

- To help students practice scanning as a selective reading skill.
- To help students understand the mock trial case in detail.
- To let students practice analyzing the character of a party in the mock trial.
- To let students use interactive listening and speaking skills for discussion as well as writing skills for taking notes.

Procedure/Instructions

1. Have students get into pairs or groups of three.
2. Guide students to manage their time in completing all tasks.
3. Walk around the classroom and monitor students' participation and progress while they work in teams.

Suggested Times 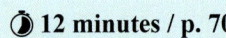 12 minutes / p. 70

Aims
- To help students understand the specifics of the mock trial case as they compare it with the facts of a precedent they read in Lesson 4.
- To let students practice interactive listening and speaking for discussion as well as writing skills for taking notes.

Procedure/Instructions
1. Tell students to work in the same pairs or groups as in the previous task.
2. Remind students that the goal of the activity is to compare specifics between the mock trial case and the Fisher case in Lesson 4.
3. Encourage students to compare the passages in Lesson 4 and Lesson 6.
4. Encourage students to focus on filling in the table with information as much as possible.

Suggested Times 🕐 13 minutes / pp. 71-72

Aims
- To help students practice scanning as a selective reading skill.
- To help students examine the case from both points of view and think critically.
- To let students practice interactive listening and speaking for discussion.

Procedure/Instructions
1. Tell students to work in the same pairs or groups as in the previous task.
2. Guide students to scan the passage on p. 71 to determine what they think is useful information.
3. Remind students that they can refer to the passage about the mock trial case on pp. 66-68 at any time.
4. Walk around the classroom and monitor students' participation and progress while they work in teams.

Suggested Times ⏱ 13 minutes / p. 73

Aims
- To help students practice scanning as a selective reading skill.
- To help students use quotations.
- To help students examine the case from both points of view and think critically.
- To let students practice interactive listening and speaking for discussion.

Procedure/Instructions
1. Tell students to work in the same pairs or groups as the previous task.
2. Encourage students to select as many quotations as possible.
3. Remind students that they can refer to the passage about the mock trial case on pp. 66-68 at any time to compare the case with the opinions from the Fisher case.
4. Walk around the classroom and monitor students' participation and progress while they work in teams.

Suggested Times ⏱ 13 minutes / p. 74

Aims
- To help students interpret the characters of both parties in the mock trial case from a creative point of view.
- To let students practice interactive listening and speaking for discussion as well as writing skills for taking notes.

Procedure/Instructions
1. Tell students to work in the same pairs or groups as the previous task.
2. Remind students that they can refer to the passage about the mock trial case on pp. 66-68 at any time.
3. Walk around the classroom and monitor students' participation and progress while they work in teams.

Unit I Lesson 7

Suggested Times 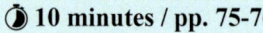 10 minutes / pp. 75-76

Aims
- To decide teams and members.
- To explore distinctions between "a lawyer" and "a counsel".
- To let students practice interactive listening and speaking for discussion.

Procedure/Instructions
1. Ask students to make groups of three or four with new members whom they did not work together with on the case analysis activities in Lesson 6.
2. Explain that this encourages students to utilize various ideas about case analyses from different groups' previous discussions when they discuss writing an oral argument script, making it possible for them to anticipate possible questions and rebuttals.
3. If they cannot make a group with entirely new members, two members in a group can be from the group of previous activities.
4. Spend 4 minutes to elect a team representative, assign parties, and decide the roles of the team.
5. Give 1 minute to read instructions on p. 75 as a class.
6. Give another 3 minutes to fill in the table on p. 76 and to have a mini discussion for the mini quiz.
7. Check answers for the mini quiz and have Q&A if necessary.

Tip: Use the mini quiz to explore distinctions between "a lawyer" and "a counsel". A lawyer can broadly refer to a law professional such as an attorney at law or a prosecutor. Meanwhile, a counsel is an advocate for a specific party at a court.

Suggested Times ⏱ 10 minutes / pp. 77-78

Aims
- To provide structural guidance.
- To help students understand the process of oral argument and sequence of their tasks at the mock trial.
- To help students understand their task.

Procedure/Instructions
1. Ask students to take a look at the flow chart of the oral argument and make sure that it is the sequence of how each team member will present.
2. As a class, read the elements of oral argument on p. 78 together, taking turns reading aloud.
3. Have Q&A in order to make sure students understand what to do at each stage/turn.

Tip: In regards to the flow chart, point out that in real oral arguments at the U. S. Supreme Court, one counsel from each party presents the entire oral argument while justices instantly engage in questioning in the middle of the oral argument. However, for our mock trial, to encourage fairness, the oral argument is divided into reasons.

E. Teacher's Manual 201

Suggested Times 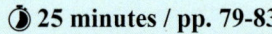 25 minutes / pp. 79-83

Aims
- To teach key expressions and styles used in actual courtroom dialogue.
- To provide an opportunity to explore how the expressions are used in a courtroom dialogue.
- To provide an opportunity to review the structure and the elements of argument in the sample dialogue.
- To let students practice collaborative reading while practicing a sample dialogue.

Procedure/Instructions
1. Ask students to sit together as a team.
2. Have a volunteer read aloud the instructions on the top of p. 79.
3. Give 3 minutes to let students read the information on p. 79 and divide the six roles in the table between the members.
4. Give 12 minutes for performing the script on pp. 80-83.
5. Walk around groups to monitor students, checking on whether or not they have any problems.
6. Have 8 minutes to share each team's reflection on the practice of performing the script.
a) Check if students recognize what mode of persuasion is used in each counsel's oral argument and if they recognize contentions, reasonings, and specific evidence or examples in each counsel's oral argument.
b) Check if students recognize other unique expressions or styles in counsels' oral arguments.
c) Have Q&A if necessary.

| Suggested Times | ⏱ 30 minutes / pp. 84-86 |

Aims

- To let students understand general strategies for preparing oral arguments.
- To let students collaborate on constructing arguments and practice oral arguments together.
- To let students prepare an oral argument as well as practice argumentative writing.
- To let students practice interactive listening and speaking for discussion.

Procedure/Instructions

1. Make sure students plan the oral argument as a team but write script and outline individually.
2. Tell students to use the instructions for preparing their oral argument according to their roles. Counsels use p. 85 and justices use p. 86.
3. Walk around the class to monitor students and to check if students have any trouble with the task.

Unit I Lesson 8

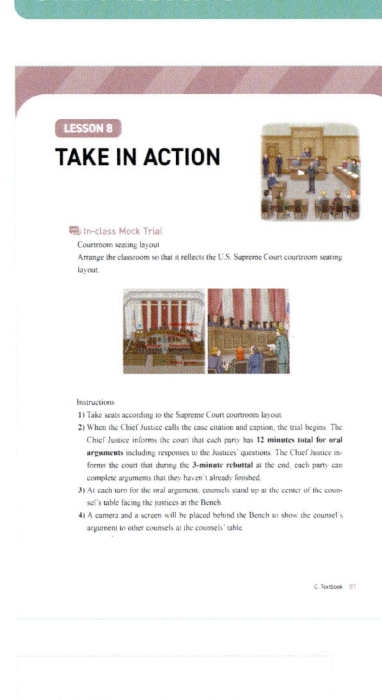

| Suggested Times | ⏱ 5 minutes / p. 87 |

Aims
- To provide clear instruction on the process of the mock trial.
- To let students imagine and understand the Supreme Court courtroom layout.

Procedure/Instructions
1. Ask students to arrange the classroom according to the image on the left.
2. Ask students to read the instructions carefully.
3. Tell students the teacher will sit in the public gallery seat.

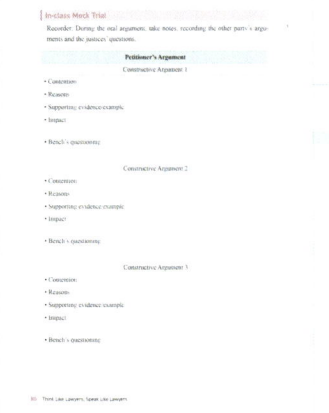

| Suggested Times | ⏱ 30 minutes / pp. 88-89 |

Aims
- To let students use all skills and strategies learned for debate in courtroom oral argument.
- To let students perform oral arguments referring to the script and outline they prepared in Lesson 7.
- To let students practice interactive listening and speaking for questioning and answering.
- To help students use listening skills while the other team performs oral arguments by taking notes.

Procedure/Instructions
1. Tell students to begin after reading the instructions on the previous page whenever they are ready.
2. Tell students in counsel teams to choose the appropriate form either on p. 88 or p. 89 according to their roles.
3. Tell students on the justices team to use both forms on p. 88 and p. 89.
4. Monitor students from a seat in the gallery.

Suggested Times ⏱ 10 minutes / pp. 90-91

Aims
- To provide an opportunity to reflect on the entire process of mock trial and the other team members' arguments.
- To provide an opportunity to review lessons especially regarding the three modes of persuasion and speech delivery.
- To let students practice interactive listening and speaking skills for discussion.

Procedure/Instructions
1. Give students 6 minutes to have a discussion as a team to complete the questionnaire on p. 90 and p. 91.
2. Ask for volunteers to share their peer feedback with the class. In the case where there are no volunteers, move on directly to the next procedure.
3. Give the class overall feedback, highlighting the strengths of the students' performances and mentioning areas in which students can improve.

Tip: Make a teacher's assessment sheet according to the criteria found in the peer feedback questionnaire.

| Suggested Times | ⏱ 10 minutes / p. 92 |

Aims
- To provide an opportunity to reflect on new learning and complexities of promoting diversity.
- To question students' own views.

Procedure/Instructions
1. Tell students to work individually.

| Suggested Times | ⏱ 20 minutes / p. 93 |

Aims
- To help students take a critical stance.
- To let students practice genre writing.
- To provide an opportunity to practice taking action for making change.

Procedure/Instructions
1. Tell students to work individually.
2. Tell students the mock trial case illuminates an actual ongoing problem in Korea.
3. Give 20 minutes to write a suggestion letter on p. 93.
4. Let students know they can change the recipient of the letter to whomever they believe has the authority to enact meaningful change.
5. Have a volunteer presenter share their writing with the class.

Unit II Lesson 1

Suggested Times ⏱ 8 minutes / p. 94

Aims

- To introduce the objectives and theme.
- To figure out students' familiarity with the theme.
- To activate students' schema.

Procedure/Instructions

1. Ask students to read the title and objectives.
2. Question students about unknown words in the title.
3. Provide the meanings of "xenophobia", "counter", and "convention".
4. Ask students to recall their college admission experience and to guess how the word "xenophobia" could be relevant to college admissions policies.

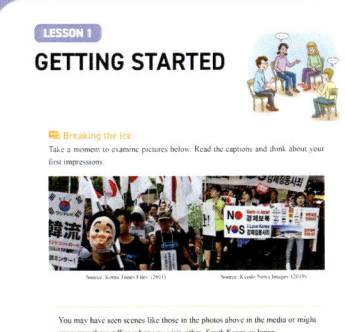

Suggested Times ⏱ 6 minutes / p. 95

Aims

- To provide an opportunity to analyze code.
- To let students practice intensive reading.

Procedure/Instructions

1. Ask students to take a look at the pictures first and ask them if they have encountered something similar in their real lives.
2. Give 2 minutes to read the written description about the picture silently.
3. Give another 3 minutes to examine the pictures and think about whether or not they feel the pictures are problematic.

E. Teacher's Manual 207

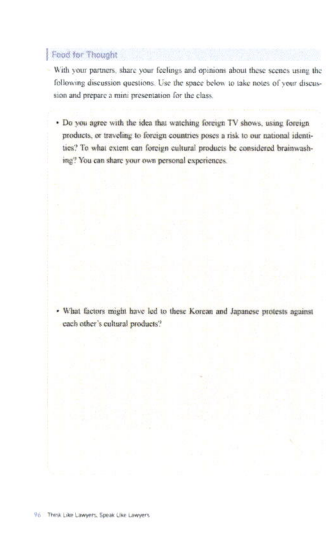

Suggested Times   ⏱ 16 minutes / p. 96

Aims

- To provide opportunities to interpret potential problematic situations relevant to students' real lives.
- To let students practice interactive listening and speaking as well as writing skills for taking notes.

Procedure/Instructions

1. Give 1 minute to read the instructions and the discussion questions in the box.
2. Have students get into pairs or groups of three.
3. Give 10 minutes for discussion and 5 minutes to share their discussion with the class.

Suggested Times   ⏱ 9 minutes / p. 97

Aims

- To introduce key concepts relevant to the theme of the unit and topics in the following lessons.
- To help students conceptualize words by analyzing code.

Procedure/Instructions

1. Tell students to work on this activity individually.
2. Ask students to read the instructions and words in the box carefully.
3. Ask students to take time to think about the pictures as they answer the questions.

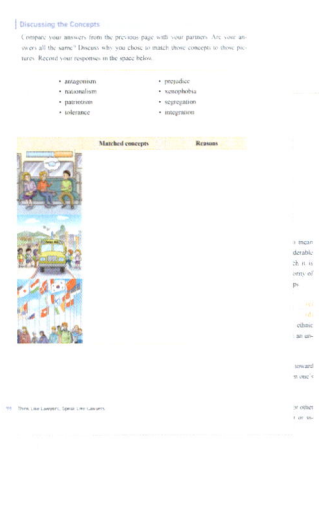

Suggested Times   ⏱ 18 minutes / pp. 98-99

Aims
- To provide an opportunity to examine how others interpret the same thing differently.
- To let students practice interactive listening and speaking as well as writing skills for taking notes.
- To check students' understanding.

Procedure/Instructions
1. Have students get into pairs or groups of three.
2. Give 8 minutes to discuss the concepts on p. 98.
3. Have 4 minutes to share the group discussion.
4. Give 3 minutes to work individually on the questions on p. 99 to review the concepts.
5. Have 3 minutes to check answers and conduct Q&A time.

Suggested Times   ⏱ 18 minutes / p. 100

Aims
- To provide opportunities to interpret potential problematic situations relevant to students' real life.
- To let students practice interactive listening and speaking for discussion as well as writing skills for taking notes.

Procedure/Instructions
1. Give 1 minute to read the instructions and the discussion questions in the box.
2. Have students get into pairs or groups of three.
3. Give 12 minutes for discussion and 5 minutes to share their discussion with the class.

E. Teacher's Manual 209

Unit II Lesson 2

Suggested Times ⏱ 10 minutes / p. 101

Aims
- To check students' general understanding about logical fallacies.
- To activate students' schema and let them witness how faulty logic makes an argument not persuasive .
- To let students practice interactive listening and speaking for discussion as well as writing skills for taking notes.

Procedure/Instructions
1. Give 1 minute to read the instructions and take a look at the picture and check students' knowledge about the word "hoax".
2. Have students get into pairs or groups of three.
3. Give 5 minutes to handle the discussion questions.
4. Give 4 minutes to share their group discussion with the class and have Q&A time.

Suggested Times    25 minutes / pp. 102-104

Aims
• To teach ten types of logical fallacies.
• To let students work in teams and provide opportunities to learn from classmates' work.
• To let students practice intensive reading and interactive listening and speaking.

Procedure/Instructions
1. Ask students to read the passages on pp. 102-104 individually. (4 minutes)
2. Divide students into 3 groups and assign three or four logical fallacies to each group.
3. Ask students to explain to group members why the example statements demonstrate a logical fallacy without restating the given definition. (5 minutes)
4. Ask students visit other groups and exchange and explain the analyses of their assigned fallacies. (10 minutes)
5. Ask students to return to their original group and brief their team members on what they learned from other groups and check to see whether or not other groups' analyses is right. (6 minutes)

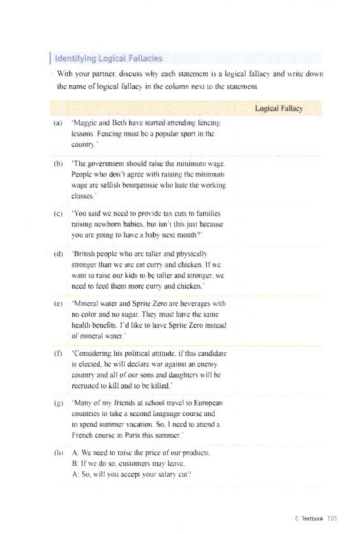

Suggested Times ⏱ 8 minutes / p. 105

Aims
- To check students' understanding and learning about logical fallacies.
- To let students practice identifying logical fallacies individually.

Procedure/Instructions
1. Tell students to work on this activity individually.
2. Give 4 minutes to solve the task.
3. Give students 4 minutes to share answers with the class and check whether or not there are different opinions regarding the answers.

Tip: The question item (b) can be answered in two ways: i) Ad hominem fallacy and ii) Straw man. Have time to share students' ideas what would be a better answer.

Suggested Times   ⏱ 25 minutes / pp. 106-108

Aims
- To teach how to counter logical fallacies.
- To let students employ knowledge about constructing arguments and strategies for countering logical fallacies.
- To let students practice interactive listening and speaking.

Procedure/Instructions
1. Give 3 minutes to read the instructions and the example dialogue on p. 106.
2. Tell students to work in pairs to construct a faulty argument and to counter a logical fallacy. Assign at least 2 logical fallacies from pp. 107-108 to each pair.
3. Give 12 minutes to work together on preparing dialogues on p. 108.
4. Make sure students try to think creatively when formulating supporting ideas and evidence for the reasons when they construct a faulty argument.
5. Make sure that students must take the roles of both speaker A and speaker B at least once.
6. Give 10 minutes for demonstrating at least one dialogue of countering a logical fallacy in front of the class.
7. Make sure to submit the rest dialogues as a written assignment.

Suggested Times ⏱ **7 minutes / p. 109**

Aims
- To provide an opportunity to review the lesson.
- To let students practice interactive listening and speaking for discussion as well as writing skills for taking notes.

Procedure/Instructions
1. Have students get into pairs or groups of three.
2. Give 5 minutes to discuss and solve the task.
3. During the last 2 minutes, ask volunteers to share their ideas from the discussion with the class.

Tip: Remind students that they can start from reviewing and restating the given definition of 10 logical fallacies on pp. 102-104.

Unit II Lesson 3

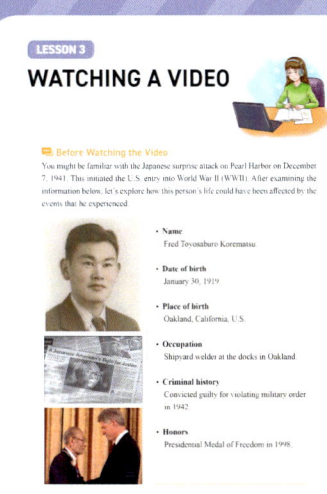

Suggested Times   ⏱ 10 minutes / p. 111

Aims
- To activate schema.
- To provide background knowledge before watching a video.
- To let students use reading skills to search for simple information and integrate information in order to preview upcoming activities.

Procedure/Instructions
1. Give 2 minutes to read the instructions and examine the pictures.
2. Ask whether or not any word needs to be explained.
3. Ask whether or not students are familiar with the person in the picture.
4. In pairs or groups of three, give 4 minutes to discuss how the information in the instruction and the box could be relevant to issues of justice.
5. Give 4 minutes to share the discussion as a class.

Suggested Times ⏱ **25 minutes / pp. 112-114**

Aims

- To introduce useful vocabulary.
- To let students distinguish differences in meaning according to context.

Procedure/Instructions

1. Tell students to work on the task on p. 112 and the first task on p. 113 in pairs or groups of three.
2. Give 8 minutes to discuss the task on p. 112.
3. Give 5 minutes to work on the first task on p. 113.
4. With the whole class, explore how the various definitions of the words "dismiss" and "motion" are related to the way they are used in a legal context.
5. Give 5 minutes to solve the second task on p. 113. Tell students to work individually on this task.
6. Check the answers together as a class and have Q&A time.
7. Give 4 minutes to solve the task on p. 114. Tell students to work individually on this task.
8. Check the answers together as a class and have Q&A time.

Suggested Times   ⏱ 15 minutes / pp. 115-116

Aims
- To let students practice intensive listening as well as writing skills for taking notes.
- To provide an opportunity to build up schema for reading activities that students will work on in Lesson 4 and Lesson 5.

Procedure/Instructions
1. Tell students to work on this activity individually.
2. Before watching the video, let students go over questions in the table on p. 115.
3. Play the video for the tasks on p. 115. (3 minutes)
4. Play only the audio for the listening comprehension quiz on p. 116. (10 minutes)
5. Check the answers as a class and have Q&A.

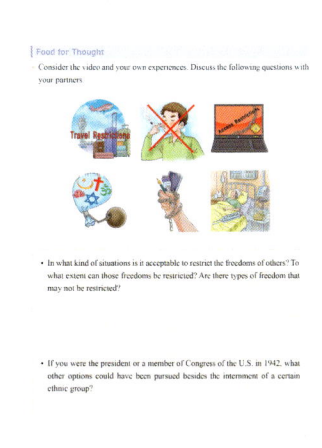

Suggested Times   ⏱ 25 minutes / p. 117

Aims
- To provide opportunities to practice critical thinking about the topic in the video.
- To let students practice interactive listening and speaking as well as writing skills for taking notes.

Procedure/Instructions
1. Have students get into pairs or groups of three.
2. Ask students to recall their personal experiences of having their freedoms restricted.
3. Remind students to take notes of their discussions.
4. Allot 15 minutes for group discussion and 10 minutes for class discussion.

Unit II Lesson 4

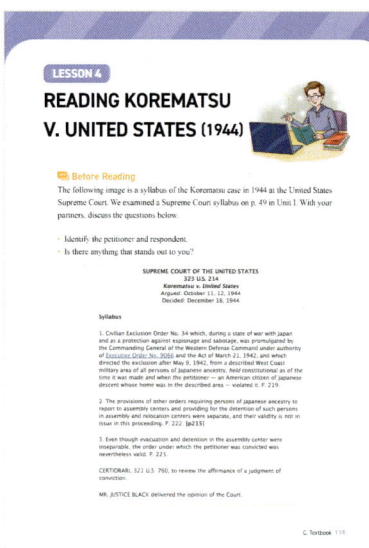

Suggested Times   ⏱ 5 minutes / p. 119

Aims

- To activate schema and to review information about court decisions.
- To let students practice interactive listening and speaking as well as writing skills for taking notes.

Procedure/Instructions

1. Have students get into pairs or groups of three.
2. Give 3 minutes to read the instructions, examine the image, and share answers for the task within their groups.
3. Check the answers as a class and see if everyone agrees to the answers.

Suggested Times  25 minutes / pp. 120-122

Aims
- To introduce useful vocabulary and key legal terms for reading.
- To prepare students to understand the main idea of the reading passage.
- To let students practice intensive reading skills as well as interactive listening and speaking skills.

Procedure/Instructions
1. Tell students to work on tasks on p. 120 in pairs or groups of three but work on the task on p. 121 individually.
2. Tell students to work as pairs or groups of three for the task on p. 122.
3. Give 7 minutes for the tasks on p. 120. Give 3 minutes for the tasks on p. 121 Check the answers as a class and have a brief Q&A.
4. Give 7 minutes for the task on p. 122.
5. Give 5 minutes to share the answers for the task on p. 122.

Suggested Times ⏱ 25 minutes / pp. 123-125

Aims
- To let students practice intensive reading.
- To prepare students for the mock trial activity that they will work on from Lesson 6 to Lesson 8.

Procedure/Instructions
1. Tell students to work on this task individually.
2. Give 12 minutes maximum to do silent reading for the reading passage on pp. 123-124. Students who finish the reading earlier can move on to the reading comprehension quiz on pp. 124-125.
3. Give another 5 minutes to solve the reading comprehension quiz. Students can refer to the reading passage.
4. Have 8 minutes to check answers as a class and for Q&A time.

Suggested Times ⏱ 20 minutes / p. 126

Aims
- To provide opportunities to employ knowledge about identifying and countering the logical fallacies learned in Lesson 2.
- To let students practice interactive listening and speaking and writing skills for taking notes and drafting an argument.

Procedure/Instructions
1. Have students get into pairs or groups of three.
2. Give 12 minutes for a discussion identifying the logical fallacy and drafting an argument to counter the logical fallacy.
3. Give 8 minutes to share the discussion with the class.

Tip: Possible answers are i) false cause, ii) hasty generalization, iii) appeal to emotion, and iv) slippery slope.

Unit II Lesson 5

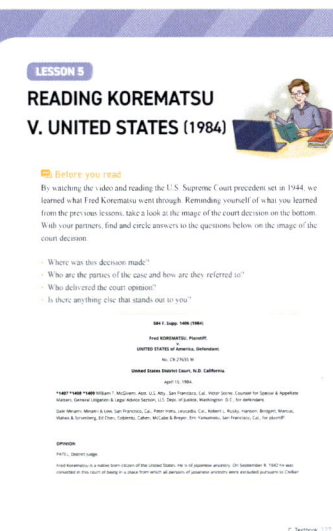

Suggested Times ⏱ 5 minutes / p. 127

Aims

- To activate schema and to distinguish the differences in the conventions of court decisions from different jurisdictions.
- To let students to use interactive listening and speaking skills as well as writing skills for taking notes.

Procedure/Instructions

1. Have students get into pairs or groups of three.
2. Give 3 minutes to read the instruction, examine the image, and share answers for the task within their groups.
3. Check the answers as a class and see if everyone agrees with the answers.

E. Teacher's Manual 221

Suggested Times　⏱ 25 minutes / pp. 128-130

Aims
- To introduce useful vocabulary and key legal terms for reading.
- To prepare students to understand the main idea of the reading passage.
- To let students practice intensive reading as well as interactive listening and speaking.

Procedure/Instructions
1. Tell students to work on tasks on p. 128 in pairs or groups of three but work on the task on p. 129 individually.
2. Tell students to work in pairs or groups of three for the task on p. 130.
3. Give 7 minutes for the tasks on p. 128. Give 5 minutes for the tasks on p. 129. Check the answers as a class and have a brief Q&A.
4. Give 7 minutes for the task on p. 130.
5. Give 5 minutes to share the answers for the task on p. 130.

Suggested Times　⏱ 12 minutes / pp. 131-132

Aims
- To let students practice intensive reading.
- To provide an opportunity to build up schema to learn knowledge for composing a rationale for the mock trial activity in the upcoming lessons.

Procedure/Instructions
1. Tell students to work on this task individually.
2. Give 12 minutes maximum to do silent reading for the reading passage on pp. 131-132. Students who finish reading earlier can move on to work on the tasks starting on p. 132.

Suggested Times ⏱ **13 minutes / pp. 132-133**

Aims
- To check students' understanding.
- To let students practice intensive reading for general comprehension and integrating information.

Procedure/Instructions
1. Tell students to work on this task individually.
2. Give 6 minutes maximum to solve the quiz. Students can refer to the reading passage.
3. Have 7 minutes to check answers as a class and to have Q&A time.

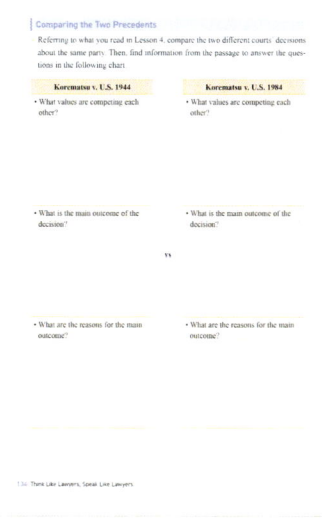

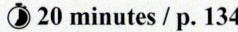

Suggested Times ⏱ **20 minutes / p. 134**

Aims
- To analyze the text by comparing the two different court decisions.
- To provide opportunities to explore how each decision constructs arguments and what critical ideas are used as reasons.

Procedure/Instructions
1. Tell students that they can work the tasks individually or in pairs.
2. Tell students that they can refer to the reading passages in the Lesson 4 and Lesson 5 while they are working on the task.
3. Give 10 minutes to solve the task on p. 134.
4. Have 10 minutes to share answers as a class and have Q&A

E. Teacher's Manual 223

Unit II Lesson 6

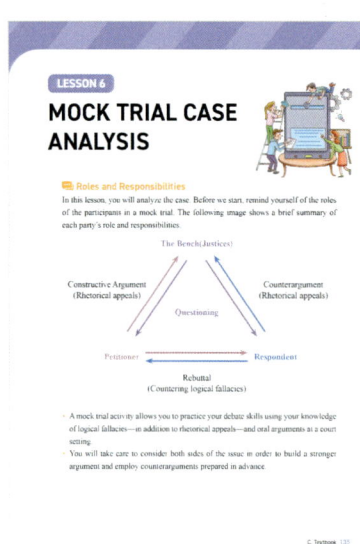

| Suggested Times | ⏱ 3 minutes / p. 135 |

Aims

- To let students prepare a mock trial activity by reviewing the purpose of the mock trial activity as well as students' roles and responsibilities in the upcoming activity.

Procedure/Instructions

1. Give 2 minutes to examine the diagram of the relationships between the parties and the descriptions of the roles under the diagram.
2. Ask students whether or not they understand at which stage they need to employ rhetorical appeals and counter logical fallacies.
3. If time allows, use a pop quiz to check students' knowledge regarding rhetorical appeals and how to counter logical fallacies.

| Suggested Times | ⏱ 12 minutes / p. 136-138 |

Aims

- To introduce the case for the mock trial activity.
- To let students to practice skimming as an intensive reading skill.

Procedure/Instructions

1. Ask students to skim through the case silently and individually.
2. While students read the case, walk around and monitor in the event that students have trouble understanding the case.
3. As a class, conduct a Q&A about the case.
4. Tell students they will return to the case during upcoming activities.

Suggested Times　　⏱ 12 minutes / pp. 138-139

Aims
- To help students practice scanning as a selective reading skill.
- To let students practice analyzing the character of a party in the mock trial.
- To help students understand the specifics of the mock trial case as they compare it with the facts of a precedent they read in Lesson 4.
- To let students practice interactive listening and speaking skills for discussion, as well as writing skills for taking notes.

Procedure/Instructions
1. Have students get into pairs or groups of three.
2. Remind students that the goal of the activity is to compare specifics between the mock trial case and the Korematsu Case in Lesson 4.
3. Encourage students to compare the passages in Lesson 4 and Lesson 6.
4. Walk around the classroom and monitor students' participation and progress while they work in teams.

E. Teacher's Manual 225

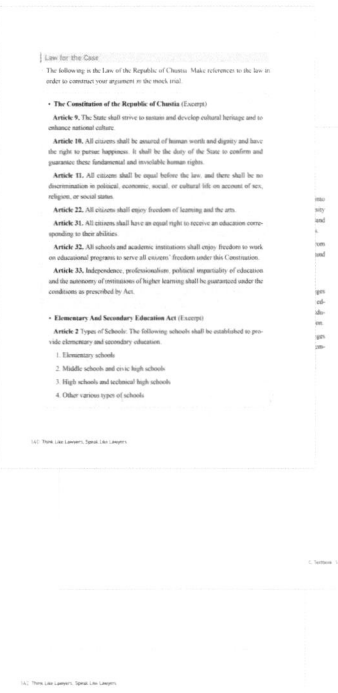

Suggested Times 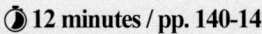 12 minutes / pp. 140-142

Aims
- To help students practice scanning as a selective reading skill.
- To help students examine the case from both points of view and think critically.
- To let students practice interactive listening and speaking for discussion.

Procedure/Instructions
1. Tell students to work in the same pairs or groups as they did on the previous task.
2. Guide students through scanning the passage on pp. 140-141 to determine what they think is useful information.
3. Remind students that they can refer to the passage about the mock trial case on pp. 136-138 at any time.
4. Walk around the classroom and monitor students' participation and progress while they work in teams.

Suggested Times   ⏱ **12 minutes / p. 143**

Aims
- To help students practice scanning as a selective reading skill.
- To help students examine the case from both points of view and think critically.
- To let students practice interactive listening and speaking for discussion.

Procedure/Instructions
1. Tell students to work in the same pairs or groups as they did in the previous task.
2. Guide students to refer to the questions in the table on p. 143 when they scan the passage about the mock trial case on pp. 136-138.
3. Guide students to think critically as they determine whether or not what either party insists is logically faulty.
4. Walk around the classroom and monitor students' participation and progress while they work in teams.

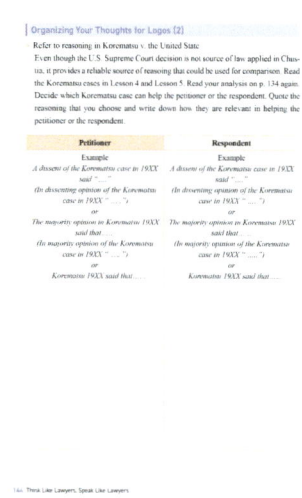

Suggested Times ⏱ 12 minutes / p. 144

Aims
- To help students practice scanning as a selective reading skill.
- To help students use quotations.
- To help students examine the case from both points of view and think critically.
- To let students practice interactive listening and speaking for discussion.

Procedure/Instructions
1. Tell students to work in the same pairs or groups as they did in the previous task.
2. Encourage students to select as many quotations as possible.
3. Remind students that they can refer to the mock trial case on pp. 136-138 at any time to compare the case and the opinions from the Korematsu cases.
4. Walk around the classroom and monitor students' participation and progress while they work in teams.

Suggested Times   ⏱ **12 minutes / p. 145**

Aims

- To help students interpret the characters of both parties in the mock trial case from a creative point of view.
- To let students practice interactive listening and speaking for discussion as well as writing skills for taking notes.

Procedure/Instructions

1. Tell students to work in the same pairs or groups as they did in the previous task.
2. Remind students that they can refer to the passage about the mock trial case on pp. 136-138 at any time.
3. Walk around the classroom and monitor students' participation and progress while they work in teams.

Unit II Lesson 7

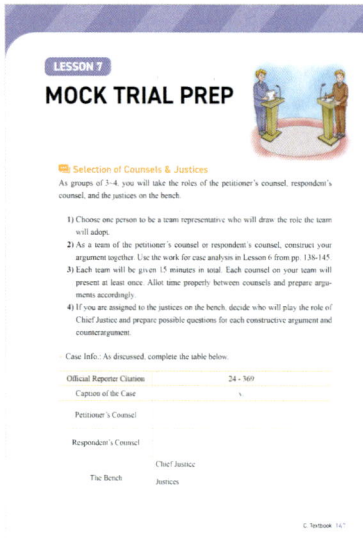

Suggested Times ⏱ 7 minutes / p. 147

Aims
- To decide teams and members.
- To let students practice interactive listening and speaking for discussion.

Procedure/Instructions
1. Ask students to make groups of three or four with new members whom they did not work together with on the case analysis activities in Lesson 6.
2. Explain that this encourages students to utilize various ideas about case analyses from different groups' previous discussions when they discuss writing an oral argument script, making it possible for them to anticipate possible questions and rebuttals.
3. If they cannot make a group with entirely new members, two members in a group can be from the same group in previous activities.
4. Spend 4 minutes to elect a team representative, assign parties, and decide the roles of the team.
5. Give another 3 minutes to read instructions and to fill in the table on p. 147.
6. Have Q&A if necessary.

Suggested Times ⏱ **5 minutes / p. 148**

Aims
- To provide structural guidance.
- To help students review the process of oral argument and sequence of their tasks at the mock trial.
- To help students understand new requirements of the elements of argument in the mock trial activity.

Procedure/Instructions
1. Ask students to take a look at the flow chart of oral argument and make sure that there are additional requirements during rebuttal.
2. Ask students whether or not they can recall the requirements of a rebuttal in Lesson 7 in Unit I.

Tip: Ask students to go back to p. 78 and remind themselves of the elements and requirements of argument.

3. Have volunteer readers and ask them to read aloud the new requirements of rebuttal on p. 148.
4. Have Q&A in order to make sure students understand what to do at each stage/turn.

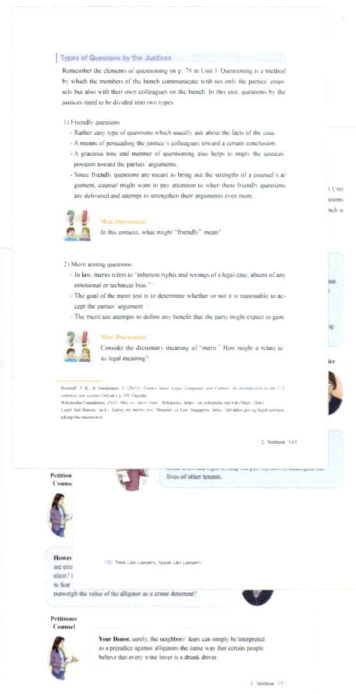

Suggested Times 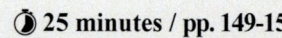 **25 minutes / pp. 149-151**

Aims
- To help students understand new requirements of the elements of argument in the mock trial activity.
- To teach students two different types of questions.
- To provide an opportunity to explore how the two types of questions are used in a courtroom dialogue.
- To let students practice collaborative reading while practicing a sample dialogue.

Procedure/Instructions
1. Ask students to sit together as a team.
2. Give 3 minutes to let students read the information on p. 149 and discuss the questions.
3. As a class, share the answers for the mini discussion questions and see if everyone agrees with the answers.
4. Give 12 minutes for performing the script on pp. 150-151. Ask students to delegate the four roles among their group members.
5. Walk around groups to monitor students, checking whether or not they have any problems.
6. Have 8 minutes to share each team's reflection on the practice of performing script.
a) Ask students whether or not they recognize the differences between two types of questions clearly.
b) Ask students what kind of other strategies they can use to deliver the two types of questions effectively and clearly and recognize those questions easily.
c) Have Q&A if necessary.

Suggested Times ⏱ 30 minutes / pp. 152-153

Aims
- To let students collaborate on constructing arguments and practicing oral arguments together.
- To let students prepare an oral argument as well as practice argumentative writing.
- To let students practice interactive listening and speaking for discussion.

Procedure/Instructions
1. Make sure students plan the oral argument as a team but write the script and outline individually.
2. Tell students to use the instructions for preparing oral arguments according to their roles.
3. Make sure students who are playing the role of counsel prepare themselves with the new requirements for rebuttal on p. 148.
4. Make sure students who are playing the role of justices prepare both types of questions on p. 149.
5. Walk around the class to monitor students and to check if students have any trouble with the task.

Unit II Lesson 8

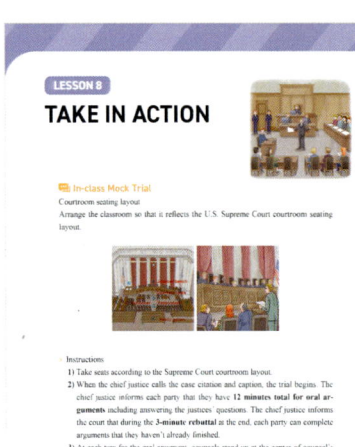

Suggested Times ⏱ 2 minutes / p. 155

Aims
- To provide clear instruction on the process of the mock trial.
- To let students imagine and understand the Supreme Court courtroom layout.

Procedure/Instructions
1. Ask students to arrange the classroom according to the image on the left.
2. Ask students to read the instructions carefully.
3. Tell students the teacher will sit in the public gallery seat.

Suggested Times ⏱ 30 minutes / pp. 156-157

Aims
- To let students use all skills and strategies learned for debate in courtroom oral argument.
- To let students perform oral arguments referring to the script and outline they prepared in Lesson 7.
- To let students practice interactive listening and speaking for questioning and answering.
- To help students use listening skills while the other team performs oral arguments by taking notes.

Procedure/Instructions
1. Tell students to begin after reading the instructions on the previous page whenever they are ready.
2. Tell students in counsel teams to choose a form either on p. 156 or p. 157 according to their roles.
3. Tell students on the justices team to use both forms on p. 156 and p. 157 for recording.
4. Monitor students' performance from a seat in the gallery.

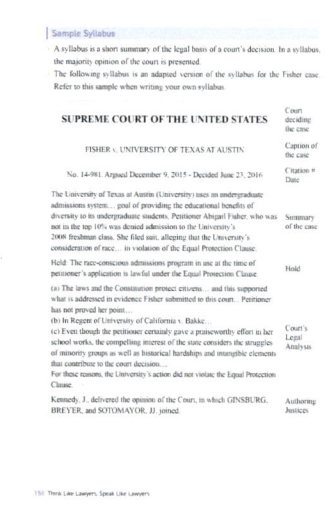

Suggested Times   ⏱ 8 minutes / p. 158

Aims

- To teach the meaning of syllabus in legal contexts.
- To let students to explore the structure and elements of a syllabus.
- To let students practice scanning as they explore the structure and elements of a syllabus.

Procedure/Instructions

1. Give 5 minutes maximum to scan the sample syllabus.
2. Check if students can identify the three modes of persuasion in the court's legal analysis of the sample syllabus.

Suggested Times   ⏱ 10 minutes / p. 159

Aims

- To provide an opportunity to review the case and oral arguments at the mock trial activity.
- To help students make an outline to organize thoughts for writing a summary.
- To help students to organize thoughts for argumentative writing containing all three modes of persuasion.
- To let student practice interactive listening and speaking for discussion.

Procedure/Instructions

1. Tell students to have a discussion with group members to compose a majority opinion.

Suggested Times ⏱ 15 minutes / pp. 160-161

Aims
- To provide an opportunity to develop one's positionality regarding the case in the syllabus.
- To let students practice genre writing.

Procedure/Instructions
1. Tell student to work individually.
2. Encourage students to refer to the outline and discussion notes on p. 159.
3. Encourage students to refer to the sample syllabus on p. 158.
4. Encourage students to refer to work they did in previous lessons for organizing thoughts for the oral argument and writing a script.

Suggested Times ⏱ 10 minutes / p. 162

Aims
- To provide an opportunity to reflect on new learning and complexities of cultural xenophobia.
- To question students' own views.

Procedure/Instructions
1. Tell students to work individually.

E. Teacher's Manual

References

Books & Journals

Brostoff, T. K., & Sinsheimer, A. (2013). *United States Legal Language and Culture: An Introduction to the U.S. common law system* (3rd ed.). Oceana.

Brown, H. D. (2007). *Teaching by principles* (3rd ed.). Pearson Longman.

Brown, H. D., & Lee, H. (2015). *Teaching by principles: An interactive approach to language pedagogy* (4th ed.). Pearson Education.

Chisholm, N. (2013). Legal Diffusion and the Legal profession: An Analysis of the Processes of American Influence on South Korea's Lawyers. *Columbia Journal of Asian Law*, 26(2), 267-298.

Crookes, G. (2013). *Critical ELT in action: Foundations, promises, praxis.* Routledge.

Garbe, W., & Stoller, F. L. (2002). *Teaching and researching reading.* Longman, Harlow.

Harmer, J. (2011). *The practice of English language teaching.* Pearson/Longman.

Menis, S. (2016). Non-traditional students and critical pedagogy: Transformative practice and the teaching of criminal law. *Teaching in Higher Education*, 22(2), 193–206. https://doi.org/10.1080/13562517.2016.1237492

Richards, J., & Rodgers, T. (2015). *Approaches and Methods in Language Teaching* (3rd ed.). Cambridge University Press.

Online Media

Brett Snider, E. (2014, January 27). *Challenging laws: 3 levels of scrutiny explained.* FindLaw. Retrieved November 4, 2022, from https://www.findlaw.com/legalblogs/law-and-life/challenging-laws-3-levels-of-scrutiny-explained/#:~:text=When%20the%20constitutionality%20of%20a,Rational%20basis%20review

Common European Framework of Reference for Languages. (1991). *The CEFR Levels.* Retrieved October 16, 2022, from https://www.coe.int/en/web/common-european-framework-reference%20languages/level-descriptions

Constitutional Court of Korea. (2019). *Case on Seoul National University's Entrance Examination Plan, 92Hun-Ma68* (1992). https://english.ccourt.go.kr/site/eng/decisions/casesearch/caseSearch.do

Holzer, J. (2023, October 10). *What is the difference between nationalism and patriotism?*. The Conversation. https://theconversation.com/what-is-the-difference-between-nationalism-and-patriotism-208170

Immigration History. (2019, September 27). *Korematsu v. United States (1984)*. https://immigrationhistory.org/item/korematsu-v-united-states-1984/

Jones, C. (2021, January 8). *Logical fallacy.* English 102 Journey Into Open. https://open.maricopa.edu/english102open/chapter/logical-fallacy/

Justia Law. (2003). *Korematsu v. United States, 323 U.S. 214 (1944)*. https://supreme.justia.com/cases/federal/us/323/214/

Justia Law. (2003). *Korematsu v. United States, 584 F. supp. 1406 (N.D. cal. 1984)*. https://law.justia.com/cases/federal/district-courts/FSupp/584/1406/2270281/

Korea Times Files. (2011). [Photograph of right-wing activists staging a rally to denounce Japan's Fuji TV for airing Korean entertainment shows and dramas]. The Korea Times. http://koreatimes.co.kr/www/news/culture/2014/02/135_152045.html.

Korea Law Translation Center. (2010). *Act on the Establishment and Management of Professional Law Schools.* Statutes of the Republic of Korea. Retrieved November 4, https://elaw.klri.re.kr/eng_service/lawView.do?hseq=38870&lang=ENG

Korea Law Translation Center. (2010). *Constitution of The Republic of Korea.* Statutes of the Republic of Korea. Retrieved November 4, 2022, https://elaw.klri.re.kr/kor_service/lawView.do?hseq=1&lang=ENG

Korea Law Translation Center. (2010). *Elementary and Secondary Education Act.* Statutes of the Republic of Korea. Retrieved November 4, https://elaw.klri.re.kr/eng_service/lawView.do?hseq=61414&lang=ENG

Korea Law Translation Center. (2010). *Higher Education Act.* Statues of the Republic of Korea. Retrieved November 4, https://elaw.klri.re.kr/eng_service/lawView.do?hseq=61316&lang=ENG

Korematsu Institute. (2021, June 19). *Fred's story.* https://korematsuinstitute.org/freds-story/

Kyodo News Images. (2019). [Photograph of protesters calling for a boycott of Japan-made products in response to Tokyo's tighter export controls]. The Japan Times. https://www.japantimes.co.jp/news/2019/08/28/national/politics-diplomacy/japan-south-korea-relations-where-did-it-all-go-wrong/

Lawrina. (2023, April 6). *Probation vs. parole: What is the difference?*. https://lawrina.org/blog/probation-vs-parole-what-is-the-difference/

Legal Aid Bureau. (n.d.). *Taking the merits test.* Ministry of Law Singapre. https://lab.mlaw.gov.sg/legal-services/taking-the-merits-test/

Legal Information Institute. (1992). *Welcome to the LII.* Legal Information Institute. Retrieved November 2, 2022, from https://www.law.cornell.edu/

Naunton, M., & Franklin, C. (n.d.). *What is meant by 'if it pleases the court' or when the judge says 'the court is not pleased with such.* Quora. Retrieved November 4, 2022, from https://www.quora.com/What-is-meant-by-if-it-pleases-the-court-or-when-the-judge-says-the-court-is-not-pleased-with-such-and-such-aside-from-the-obvious-inference

Oyez Project. (1980). *Fisher v. University of Texas.* Oyez. https://www.oyez.org/cases/2015/14-981

Oyez Project. (1980). *Korematsu v. United States.* Oyez. https://www.oyez.org/cases/1940-1955/323us214

Park, H. J. (2022). *Is CLP possible for Korean law professionals to develop their multicultural competence? A critical study of Korean lawyers' views towards multiculturalism.* ScholarSpace. https://scholarspace.manoa.hawaii.edu/items/ad2370d4-38ce-4333-8803-cd2d85046c50

Quimbee. (2021, September 7.) *Fisher v. University of Texas (Fisher II) Case Brief Summary* I Law Case Explained [Video]. Youtube. https://www.youtube.com/watch?v=e6J1GNXzh-o&t=21s

Quimbee. (2023, October 13.) *Korematsu v. United States Case Brief Summary* I Law Case Explained [Video]. Youtube. https://www.youtube.com/watch?v=5O8Xsda2AXk

Rennemeyer, A. (2021, July 7). *Logical fallacies–definition and fallacy examples.* freeCodeCamp.org. https://www.freecodecamp.org/news/logical-fallacies-definition-fallacy-examples/

Renee Booker L. (2023, November 20). *When is a judge referred to as "Your honor"?* My Law Questions. https://www.mylawquestions.com/when-is-a-judge-referred-to-as-your-honor.htm

Ridgeway, B. (2020, March 23). *Debate skills Topic #1* [Lecture notes on resource allocation]. Graduate School of Teaching Foreign Languages TESOL, Ewha Womans University. https://cyber.ewha.ac.kr/

Ridgeway, B. (2020, April 6). *Rhetoric Topic #3* [Lecture notes on resource allocation]. Graduate School of Teaching Foreign Languages TESOL, Ewha Womans University. https://cyber.ewha.ac.kr/

Shatz, I. (n.d.). *Logical Fallacies: What They Are and How to Counter Them.* Effectiviology. https://effectiviology.com/guide-to-logical-fallacies/#How_to_counter_logical_fallacies

The Administrative Office of the U.S. Courts. (n.d.). *Facts and case summary - korematsu v. U.S.* United States Courts. (n.d.). https://www.uscourts.gov/educational-resources/educational-activities/facts-and-case-summary-korematsu-v-us

The Law Dictionary. (n.d.). Black's Law Dictionary-Free Online Legal Dictionary. Retrieved October 26, 2022, from https://thelawdictionary.org/

Wikimedia Foundation. (2023, May 6). *Merit (law).* Wikipedia. https://en.wikipedia.org/wiki/Merit_(law)

Think Like Lawyers, Speak Like Lawyers
Preparing for U.S. Law School

1판 1쇄 발행   2024년 12월 27일

지 은 이 | 박희진
펴 낸 이 | 김진수
펴 낸 곳 | 한국문화사
등   록 | 제1994-9호
주   소 | 서울시 성동구 아차산로49, 404호 (성수동1가, 서울숲코오롱디지털타워3차)
전   화 | 02-464-7708
팩   스 | 02-499-0846
이 메 일 | hkm7708@daum.net
홈페이지 | http://hph.co.kr

ISBN 979-11-6919-277-4 93740

· 이 책의 내용은 저작권법에 따라 보호받고 있습니다.
· 잘못된 책은 구매처에서 바꾸어 드립니다.
· 이 책에서 인용한 일부 이미지를 원저작의 사전 이용 허락을 얻지 못한 점 양해 부탁드립니다.
  추후에라도 저작권과 관련한 문의를 주시면 성실히 응하겠습니다. (e-mail: hjpark21@hawaii.edu)
· 책값은 뒤표지에 있습니다.

오류를 발견하셨다면 이메일이나 홈페이지를 통해 제보해주세요.
소중한 의견을 모아 더 좋은 책을 만들겠습니다.